TOUCHE ROSS'S

Management buy-outs

TOUCHE ROSS'S

Management buy-outs
Second edition

MIKE WRIGHT,
JAMES NORMAND AND KEN ROBBIE

WOODHEAD-FAULKNER

NEW YORK   LONDON   TORONTO   SYDNEY   TOKYO   SINGAPORE

Published by Woodhead-Faulkner Limited,
Simon & Schuster International Group,
Fitzwilliam House, 32 Trumpington Street,
Cambridge CB2 1QY, England
in association with Touche Ross & Co,
a member of DRT International
Hill House, 1 Little New Street
London EC4A 3TR, England

First published 1987
Second edition 1990

© Spicer and Pegler Ltd 1987
© Touche Ross & Co 1990

British Library Cataloguing in Publication Data
Wright, Michael 1952–
Touche Ross's management buy-outs.–2nd ed.
1. Great Britain. Companies. Buy–outs by managers
I. Title II. Normand, James III. Robbie, Ken IV. Spicer
& Pegler's management buy-outs
658.16
ISBN 0–85941–717–4

Designed by Geoff Green
Typeset by Pentacor PLC, High Wycombe, Bucks.
Printed in Great Britain by BPCC Wheatons Ltd, Exeter

Contents

vi

Preface

The second edition of this book appears as we enter the second decade of management buy-outs in the United Kingdom. The first ten years of the phenomenon were marked by major changes in the value, volume and sources of deals and finance. In the three years since the first edition was published, we have witnessed the rise and currently the fall of the very large buy-out, the establishment of the buy-in market, the extensive use of buy-outs to take quoted firms private, the development of mezzanine funding and the appearance of the hostile buy-in bid for publicly quoted companies. The continental European buy-out market has also displayed rapid development, especially in France but increasingly in other countries. This edition incorporates these recent developments in several ways. The first chapter has been completely revised so as to present a more detailed analysis of trends in buy-outs and buy-ins in the United Kingdom, United States and continental Europe. This chapter draws extensively on information kept on the Centre for Management Buy-out Research database, which in the last three years has developed as the only comprehensive source of information on buy-outs and buy-ins. The second chapter has been extended to deal in more detail with the issues involved in buy-outs of quoted companies and of those involving public-sector activities.

Chapters 3 to 7 have been strengthened to take account of the implications of the recent trends in the market on negotiating and structuring management buy-outs. Chapters 3 and 8 present updated survey material on post-buy-out conditions which picks up the changed circumstances in which buy-outs occurred from the mid-1980s to the end of the decade. In Chapter 8 also, a major development has been the greater attention to the wider range of exit routes which have recently developed in addition to stock-market flotations and sale to other groups. Recapitalisations, secondary buy-outs and buy-ins seem set to increase in importance.

Two of the case studies in Chapter 9 have been replaced with commentaries dealing with buy-outs of local-authority services and cross-border activities. The Metsec case has been updated to encompass post-flotation issues and a case study of a management buy-in has been included for the first time. A new concluding chapter has been added which summarises recent developments and considers prospects for buy-outs in the 1990s.

It is not only the buy-out market that has changed since the first edition appeared. Spicer and Pegler became Spicer & Oppenheim and then merged with Touche Ross. Two out of the three contributing authors have also changed. James Normand, a Director of Touche Ross Corporate Finance brings a wealth of expertise in completing buy-out and buy-in deals. Ken Robbie brings the unparalleled experience of having assembled and analysed details of over 4,000 deals, as well as having been directly involved in selling several subsidiaries of a group as management buy-outs.

As before, we would like to record our thanks to several colleagues for helpful insights and discussions: Brian Chiplin, Steve Thompson, Patrick Harrex, Peter Miles, Adam Mills, Bob Willott, Michael Cumming, Clive McClintock, Maurice O'Brien, Pierre Dupouy, Catherine Heuze, Johan Bruining and Matthias Graeper. Grateful thanks are also due to the management teams of Metsec, City Centre Leisure, Vickers Furniture and Innoxa for their co-operation in allowing us to report their buy-out and buy-in experiences. Karen Stretton provided very helpful research experience and Sandra Mienczakowski worked wonders in typing the manuscript.

Introduction

Although this book is written as an integrated whole, readers may find certain parts to be of more direct relevance to them than others. Those wishing to obtain an overview of the development of the management buy-out and buy-in market-place in the United Kingdom, United States and continental Europe are referred to Chapters 1 and 2 respectively. Chapter 2 also addresses in detail the buy-out as a corporate strategy option, including divestment by large groups, buy-outs of companies quoted on the stock market and privatisation of public-sector activities.

Readers contemplating or involved in the negotiations for a management buy-out should find Chapters 3 to 7 of most relevance. Chapter 3 deals with the appraisal of the business, with particular emphasis being placed upon financial issues. A full actual case is used to illustrate the financial preparation required in a buy-out proposal. The development of the various types of finance for buy-outs is introduced in Chapter 1 and dealt with in detail in Chapter 4, whilst Chapter 5 discusses the important problem of structuring the financial package. Buy-outs can involve complex and delicate negotiations with vendors and financing institutions, and it is important that management secure a deal which is the most advantageous available. The issue of negotiations is addressed in Chapter 6. Successful completion requires important legal and taxation issues to be dealt with. If not handled correctly the buy-out may trigger taxation liabilities and legal action. Chapter 7 examines these crucial aspects of the deal.

Those involved in negotiations as well as those who have already completed a buy-out need to prepare for what happens after the euphoria surrounding the transfer of ownership has subsided. The main issues to be dealt with concern post-buy-out consolidation of the business, growth and strategy into the longer term and eventual exit by both the management team and financing institutions. These issues are addressed in Chapter 8.

The experience of others who have successfully achieved a buy-out provides helpful insights for those still in the process: Chapter 9 presents case studies of three actual buy-outs and one buy-in which also serve to illustrate many of the general points covered in the main body of the book. The cases cover a buy-out arising on divestment of a UK subsidiary, the buy-out of local authority leisure services, the buy-out of some of the UK and French activities of a larger group, and the buy-in of a family owned firm.

CHAPTER 1

The buy-out market-place

With origins going back as far as the beginning of capitalism itself, UK buy-outs became a significant part of the overall mergers and acquisitions market at the beginning of the 1980s. Essentially, a buy-out occurs when the ownership of a firm is transferred to a new set of shareholders among whom the incumbent management are a significant element, usually having been key to initiating the deal. The firm becomes a private independent company, with outside funding normally in the form of a mixture of equity, provided by various development-capital firms, and debt, provided by banks. From the mid-1980s onwards the United Kingdom has seen rapid growth in the phenomenon of management buy-ins, where an external management team, sometimes in conjunction with interal managers, effect a transfer of ownership with similar forms of institutional financial support.

There are important practical differences between buy-outs and buy-ins. With a buy-out, the target company is readily identified but there may be question marks over management's capabilities. In the case of a buy-in, a skilled management team may be available but matching it with the appropriate company to buy into may be difficult. However, there are sufficiently common characteristics concerning the requirements for assessing the viability of the target, negotiating the deal and funding the transaction for buy-outs and buy-ins to be examined together.

This chapter provides an overview of trends in both buy-outs and buy-ins in the United Kingdom, United States and Europe. Greatest attention is addressed to the United Kingdom in terms of the numbers and types of deal being completed as well as developments in financing techniques.

UK Buy-out and Buy-in Trends

Regular monitoring of the buy-out and buy-in market in the United Kingdom and elsewhere is carried out by the Centre for Management Buy-out Research (CMBOR). Through surveys of financing institutions, searches of the financial press and annual reports of major companies, the Centre maintains the only comprehensive database of buy-outs and buy-ins.

The beginnings of an active market were seen at the end of the 1970s. The resurgence of the concept of entrepreneurship, encouraged by the philosophical stance of the newly elected Conservative government, meant that managers were becoming more willing to run their own businesses. The desire of existing owners to sell, either as part of a need to restructure a larger group or because of a desire to retire, provided the opportunity for managers to purchase the company in which they were then employed rather than face the riskier venture of starting up a completely new firm. The growing number of venture-capital firms, established in the wake of the Wilson Committee Report and encouraged by the new entrepreneurial environment, provided a source of funds and expertise which enabled the first buy-outs to be completed. The economic spur to buying out was further enhanced by the deep recession which began in 1981, causing a tremendous increase in receiverships and a radical appraisal of the structure of firms. Buy-outs offered the possibility of job-saving for those firms in crisis situations, either in or close to receivership, through the purchase of a viable set of assets. Groups wishing to divest under-performing subsidiaries or requiring to raise cash needed elsewhere in the business quickly, often found management teams to be the only willing buyers at an acceptable price in a period of few interested external bidders given the widespread downturn in corporate profitability and need for capacity rationalisation.

Tortuous ways around initial legal problems were pioneered in the late 1970s by ICFC but subsequent relaxations in the legal framework, particularly following Section 42 of the Companies Act 1981 (now consolidated in the 1985 Act) relating to the ability for a firm to give financial assistance for borrowings (see Chapter 7) made it significantly easier to complete buy-out transactions. The ability to devise schemes which could surmount the legal barriers prior to 1981 gave those advisers and financing institutions who entered the market early an important competitive advantage which has helped them to sustain their market presence throughout the 1980s.

The coming together of all these factors attracted more advisers and institutions into the market increasing the options available, reduced the cost and complexity of completing transactions, and provided the base to seek further deals. As a result, rapid growth in the market occurred, with over 100 buy-outs completed for the first time in 1981 and over 200 in 1982 (see Table 1.1). However, in 1983 and 1984 numbers of buy-outs levelled out against a slowly rising total value of transactions.

Major developments were seen in 1985 with the buy-out market exceeding £1 billion for the first time and the number of buy-ins becoming significant, although their total value was still quite small. This marked shift upwards in the market was helped by several financing factors, most notably the development on the equity side of specialist funds and syndication techniques, and the entry of US institutions willing to provide large amounts of debt and enabled much larger deals to be concluded including those of listed companies (the first being Haden in 1985). Additionally the supply of companies was changing. A number of large groups were extending post-recession restructuring to include both the *shift* of core activities in addition to the disposal of peripheral elements. These moves produced much larger divestments of divisions and subsidiaries valued at several tens of millions of pounds. Financing

Table 1.1 UK management buy-outs and buy-ins

	Buy-outs			Buy-ins		
Year	Number	Value (£m.)	Average value (£m.)	Number	Value (£m.)	Average value (£m.)
1981	145	193	1.3	5	11	2.1
1982	238	348	1.5	8	316	39.5
1983	234	364	1.6	8	8	1.1
1984	238	403	1.7	5	3	0.7
1985	261	1,141	4.4	29	39	1.3
1986	313	1,188	3.8	49	297	6.1
1987	344	3,220	9.4	89	307	3.5
1988	373	3,717	10.0	105	1,226	11.7
1989Q2	182	1,838	10.1	63	390	6.2

Source: CMBOR is an Independent Research Centre founded by Touche Ross and Barclays Development Capital Ltd at The University of Nottingham.

techniques were developed to enable underwriting of deals and speedier response to be achieved. These moves were necessary if buy-outs were to succeed in increasingly frequent bidding against trade buyers. Such groups were becoming more acquisitive with the end of the recession and the recovery of corporate profitability. Despite these financing developments, the buy-out markets saw little growth in value in 1986, although numbers rose by one-sixth. Buy-out teams were faced increasingly with the high price–earnings ratios that could be paid by external bidders. The ability to service the high levels of debt and cumulative dividends associated with buy-out financing structures and the need to meet equity providers return targets meant in general that buy-out teams could pay less than outside bidders who were usually able to fund a purchase from resources elsewhere in the group or by issuing shares. This, however, helped to generate part of the reason for the substantial growth in the numbers and values of buy-ins in 1986/7. Some institutions may see better opportunities available for achieving target rates of return through investment in buy-ins of companies requiring restructuring which could be acquired at lower price–earnings ratios. By 1987 the acceptability of the buy-in was seen in the first buy-in of a division of a quoted company (United Precision Industries from RHP). Despite the extreme competition from corporate acquirers the value of the buy-out market increased almost threefold in 1987 as the large specialist funds came into their own. The availability of equity funding and aggressive pricing by debt providers, both UK and foreign, wishing to establish strong market presences meant that buy-out teams were more able to compete against external bidders and that much larger and more highly leveraged deals than hitherto could be financed, most notably MFI-Hygena for £717.5m. The uncertainty caused by the stock market crash of October 1987 however led to a six-month period of inactivity at the larger end of the market.

The recovery of the market in the last three quarters of 1988 meant that the combined total of buy-outs and buy-ins almost reached £5 billion, an increase of 40 per cent over 1987. Buy-out value rose 15.4 per cent, whilst that for buy-ins increased over fourfold. Not only were significantly more very large transactions for prices in excess of £100m. being completed, but a marked increase in the number of buy-outs for prices in excess of £10m. was also observed (Table 1.2). In 1988 16 per cent of buy-outs were for prices of at least £10m., compared to 9.5 per cent the previous year. The proportion of the total buy-out market value accounted

Table 1.2 Management buy-outs over £10m.
in funding 1981–1989Q2

Year	£10–25m.	£25–100m.	£100m.	Total (£m.)	Prop. of mkt (%)
1981	2	1	0	55	28.5
1982	3	2	0	144	41.4
1983	5	3	0	186	51.1
1984	3	3	0	156	38.7
1985	12	8	1	877	76.9
1986	14	8	1	698	58.8
1987	8	12	8	2,700	83.9
1988	24	18	8	3,150	83.9
1989Q2	10	11	5		

Source: CMBOR.

for by deals over £10m. is especially striking. Over four-fifths of market value for 1987 and 1988 was related to this upper end of the market. More larger buy-ins are also being transacted, but as yet numbers are some way below those for buy-outs reflecting the different stages of development of the two market sectors. Developments in the sources of buy-out, on which attention is now focused, help explain the shifts in size of buy-outs in recent years. In the first half of 1989 total volume remained buoyant, although the number of buy-outs fell for the first time since 1983. The completion of the Magnet buy-out and the hostile Isosceles buy-in of Gateway in the third quarter meant that by the end of the year total market value had risen to 27.5 billion.

Sources of Buy-outs and Buy-ins

The wide variety of buy-out and buy-in sources emphasises the diversity of the UK market-place. Much of the impetus for buy-outs in the early 1980s was the desire to create viable enterprises from those companies entering receivership, victims of a severe recession. This restructuring involved either the re-starting of independent firms, often in much reduced form, or the continuation as independent companies of viable subsidiaries of insolvent parent companies. According to the CMBOR database, over 14 per cent of buy-outs came from these sources in 1982 (Table 1.3). With the ending of the recession and the growth of other sources of buy-out, receivership sources have become less important, accounting for only 0.6 per cent of transactions in 1989.

The most important source of buy-out has always been divestment

Table 1.3 Sources of management buy-outs: number (%)

Source	Pre-1982	1982	1983	1984	1985	1986	1987	1988	1989Q2	Total
Receivership	12.56	14.28	7.04	9.00	2.15	1.73	0.65	1.98	0.57	5.02
UK parent	59.16	62.76	66.33	63.00	61.37	59.52	51.46	51.85	60.92	58.58
Foreign parent	14.14	10.20	11.06	12.50	10.02	13.84	10.68	9.97	5.17	11.11
Family ownership	10.99	8.67	11.06	12.50	21.03	19.38	25.24	29.34	27.01	19.53
Privatisation	3.14	4.08	4.52	2.00	3.00	4.84	10.68	4.84	4.02	4.97
Going private	0	0	0	0	0.43	0.69	1.29	1.71	2.30	0.79
Total	100	100	100	100	100	100	100	100	100	100
Number	191	196	199	200	233	289	309	351	174	2,151

Source: CMBOR.

from UK parents, initially because of significant recessionary pressure to restructure. More recently, substantial divestment activity is occurring as groups are effecting more considered policies concerning the strategic directions they wish to pursue in the light of their current strengths and weaknesses, and market conditions both in terms of growth prospects and the nature of competition. To some extent, a life-cycle effect may be observed as groups seek to dispose of earlier acquisitions which no longer fit new strategies. This process is also producing a relatively small number of very large divestments as some groups not only narrow down to core businesses but also shift the emphasis of their main activities.

For similar reasons, foreign-based parents have also been a significant source of buy-outs throughout the 1980s. The management and financial problems involved in controlling subsidiaries which are geographically distant from the parent may be an important reason for sale. However, in the first half of 1989, foreign divestments were at their lowest-ever share of the market.

The relative position of divestment has declined throughout the period as other sources have become more important. From 1987 buy-outs of privately owned and family firms have been at record levels. As will be seen subsequently, this type of firm has offered significant opportunities for buy-outs in continental Europe.

The UK government's programme of privatisation through stock market flotations has received a great deal of attention. However, there have also been well over 100 transfers of ownership from the public to the private sector by means of buy-outs. Throughout the 1980s some 5 per cent of buy-outs have occurred on privatisation, with more than 10 per cent being from this source in 1987 as a result of the break-up of National Bus. The variety of forms which buy-outs from the public sector may take provides an important extension to the scope of both state and local government privatisation policies and are returned to in more detail in Chapter 2.

Buy-outs of firms quoted on a stock market, 'going privates', have been a key feature of the US market for many years, as will be seen below. In the United Kingdom they only began to make their appearance in 1985 with the successful completion of the buy-out of Haden. Since then numbers have only slowly increased with this part of the market becoming of more interest after the crash of October 1987 and several high-profile deals being completed in 1989. Growing interest amongst institutions, particularly US banks, to complete such deals, which tend to be considerably larger than the average buy-out, have been an important feature. These buy-outs do, however, raise a number of contentious issues addressed in more detail in Chapter 2.

Buy-in sources are most usefully divided into private and public companies. In a private buy-in an outside team together with their financial backers generally acquire the whole of the equity of an unquoted company. Private buy-ins have for the most part so far in the United Kingdom been of private independent firms. Since 1987 a number of important divestment buy-ins, together with several from the public sector and receivership, have been recorded. Significant growth in these types of buy-ins has, however, yet to occur. Public buy-ins concern the purchase of an effective controlling equity stake, though not necessarily a majority one, in a quoted company. Those managers and financiers involved in these types of transaction may wish to avoid a level of equity-holding which would automatically trigger a stock exchange bid.

Up to 1985, private buy-in numbers were considerably in excess of those for their public counterparts (Table 1.4). However significant growth in the buy-in market in 1986 was marked by the majority of deals involving publicly quoted firms, and with a fairly even distribution in 1987, reflecting the very strong stock market in evidence up to October 1987. The relative positions were sharply reversed from 1988 as the weaker stock-market conditions made this form of buy-in less attractive, especially for those wishing to use the buy-in target as a vehicle for acquisitive activity through the issue of shares.

The relative positions in terms of value have varied quite dramatically. In 1982 the Woolworth/Paternoster public buy-in easily overshadowed all others, producing a total public buy-in value for the year which was 99 per cent of the total for this market sector. The sharp growth in activity in 1986 noted above meant that four-fifths of the market by value was accounted for by stock market buy-ins as against a little over a half in the previous year. In

Table 1.4 Source of management buy-ins (%) (numbers)

	Pre-1982	1982	1983	1984	1985	1986	1987	1988	1989Q2	All years
Private	66.7	50.0	75.0	80.0	75.9	46.9	51.7	73.3	81.0	65.5
Public	33.3	50.0	25.0	20.0	24.1	53.1	48.3	26.7	19.0	34.5
Total (%)	100	100	100	100	100	100	100	100	100	100
Number	9	8	8	5	29	49	89	105	63	365

Source: CMBOR.

1987 the growth in size of private buy-ins and the reduction in size of the public market led to a little under two-thirds of market value being contributed by private deals. The substantial growth in the market in 1988 observed earlier saw public buy-ins once more taking a little more than 50 per cent of market value. As a result the average size of public buy-in in 1988 was £21.8m. as against £8.9m. for their private counterparts. However, the private buy-in of Cope Allman at £265m. and the £446.8m. Lowndes Queensway public buy-in (achieved against an incumbent management team) had a substantial influence on the size of each part of the market. The gap in average value widened further in 1989 as a result of the Isosceles public buy-in.

Industrial and Regional Distributions

In the United Kingdom, both buy-outs and buy-ins are widespread across industrial sectors. However, there are some notable differences between the two types of transaction. In particular, buy-ins are much more prevalent in distribution and service sectors. Almost a quarter of buy-ins are to be found in distribution, compared with half this proportion for buy-outs.

Regional distributions of buy-outs and buy-ins also display some differences (Table 1.5). All buy-ins are relatively less well represented than buy-outs, in particular in Yorkshire, Humberside and Scotland, and to a lesser extent East Anglia. Buy-ins are markedly more in evidence in relative terms in the East Midlands, and to a lesser degree in the South-East, North-West and West Midlands.

Table 1.5 Regional distribution of buy-ins and buy-outs to end 1989 (%)

Region	All buy-ins	All buy-outs	All firms
South East	41.74	36.96	33.9
East Anglia	1.56	3.79	4.0
South West	6.47	7.06	9.6
West Midlands	13.17	11.61	8.5
East Midlands	8.26	5.83	6.8
Yorkshire/Humberside	6.25	9.36	7.7
North West	9.60	8.25	9.3
North	2.68	2.76	4.0
Wales	4.02	3.32	5.2
Scotland	6.03	10.55	7.5
N. Ireland	0.22	0.51	3.5
Total	100	100	100
Number	448	2,351	

Source: CMBOR.

About half of public buy-ins have their head offices in the South-East, and are relatively well represented in comparison with private buy-ins in the West Midlands and Wales. Private buy-ins are relatively under-represented compared to buy-outs in Yorkshire and Humberside and Scotland. In comparison with the stock of all firms across the regions, both buy-outs and buy-ins occur to a greater extent than might be expected in the South-East and the West Midlands.

Financing Developments

Unlike the US market, the venture- and development-capital industry has played a key role in the growth of UK buy-outs. Typically, a buy-out will be financed by a mixture of equity and debt instruments. Venture- and development-capital parts of the main London clearing banks, Barclays Development Capital, County NatWest Ventures, Lloyd's Development Capital and Midland Montagu Ventures, developed from the late 1970s onwards. Together with the longer-established 3i, and specialists such as Candover, CIN, ECI, Charterhouse Development Capital and Citicorp Venture Capital, these institutions took leading roles in putting together buy-out deals. These firms still figure among the leading group of buy-out financiers, though with developments in the size of the market and the variety of deals newer institutions have established a strong market presence. Venture- and development-capital firms engage in other forms of entrepreneurial financing besides buy-outs, such as start-up funding and second-round financing. However, the number of opportunities available and the generally lower risk for satisfactory returns has greatly influenced the amount of buy-out funding in venture-capital firms' portfolios. In 1988, buy-outs accounted for 282 financings (21 per cent of the total) worth £733m. (56 per cent of total value) by members of the British Venture Capital Association.

Developments in the market have shifted the forms of many venture capitalists' interests towards larger deals, leaving the very small end of the market to be covered by clearing-bank finance, smaller local venture-capital providers, BES funds and public-sector bodies. The importance of BES funds for buy-outs is declining as changes in government policy have made it more attractive for this type of fund to target residential assured tenancies. Also at the smaller end of the market, Enterprise Boards and Development Agencies have more recently developed a more vigorous commercial approach to their investment policies, going beyond their original job-preservation objectives.

The development of the buy-out market in the late 1980s was marked by the ability to complete large transactions so that the value rather than just the number of deals led by institutions became a key indicator of the relative importance of institutions. On this basis, Bankers Trust, Baring Capital Investors, Phildrew Ventures, Schroder Ventures, Electra, Prudential Venture Managers, Samuel Montague and MAM/Warburg may be added to the above list of providers of funds.

Specialist buy-out funds, which as noted earlier developed from 1985 to avoid the problems of equity syndication, made a significant advance in the market from 1987 onwards. Specialist funds, some of which can also invest in non-buy-out opportunities, rely on a number of institutions and wealthy individuals agreeing to commit a certain amount of money, so that when a large deal is identified, funds can be drawn down at short notice, so avoiding the delays inherent in negotiating a syndicate of institutions. In the period from 1987 to mid-1989, a little over £1bn. was raised in nine specialist funds. BZW, Charterhouse, Candover and Schroders raised second funds in the period, as they were able to invest their first ones within a short period of time. Some institutions earmarked internal funds for specific segments of the market, whilst others may be able to syndicate a buy-out internally with other parts of a larger financial group. These routes can also achieve speed in completing a deal through the provision of bridging finance for the whole of the purchase prices. The buy-out so funded may be termed a 'bought deal' and the lead underwriting institutions may sell down tranches or strips of finance to equity, mezzanine and debt providers.

The attractions of specialist funds for investors depend heavily upon the ability to realise the investment portfolio at attractive rates within the life of the fund. Various control devices may be introduced to ensure that exit via a stock market flotation or trade sale are achieved within a given period of time which would enable investors' target internal rates of return to be achieved. These aspects are returned to in later chapters.

In respect of bought deals, lead institutions need to be confident that subsequent syndication will be feasible. Generally speaking, this is not a problem but the stock market crash of 1987 and the period of very high UK interest rates in 1989 and their effects upon certain sectors of the economy made potential investors highly cautious about the ability of some buy-out candidates to service their financing commitments and led to syndication difficulties in a small number of very large deals.

As well as the earlier involvement of Citicorp, since 1985 US banks have been active investors and deal arrangers in the UK buy-out market, particularly in the arrangement of debt facilities in the larger deals.

The growing involvement of continental European banks and Japanese banks is also a noteworthy development, although the latter lag behind the former in arranging the debt side of deals. Some have moved from being just providers of finance to the role of underwriters. UK banks have also become more involved in the provision of debt in larger deals with the establishment of dedicated units to lead the debt side of buy-out funding and the integration of their various buy-out financing activities at this end of the market with Bank of Scotland and Standard Chartered having particularly significant roles. These developments in the senior debt market appear to have slowed the development of the mezzanine debt market.

The increasing price–earnings ratios paid for buy-outs and the greater focus on cash-flow generation potential of target firms, rather than just asset-backing, are closely linked to the growth in mezzanine or intermediate finance. These are the forms of finance which may be introduced into buy-out structures between pure equity and senior fully secured debt. Since the very beginning of the development of the UK buy-out market various forms of 'quasi-equity', such as preference shares, have commonly been the main type of mezzanine instrument in UK buy-outs. The newer type of mezzanine is seen as 'quasi-debt' ranking in one or more layers according to different levels of perceived risk after senior secured debt, with a higher interest rate and often carrying equity warrants to compensate for the increased risk. Mezzanine debt is not necessarily totally unsecured but with an overall return below that for pure equity. Senior mezzanine may offer a high yield but no equity kicker, junior mezzanine may carry equity warrants but a zero coupon, and various other options are available between these polar positions, leading to multiple mezzanine layers in some very large deals.

Mezzanine may be used where there are too few assets to enable sufficient secured debt to be provided and/or where the amount of equity that would have to be used to replace debt means that the returns to equity providers would be diluted to unacceptable levels.

Hence, mezzanine may be used to bridge a financing gap, to enable deals to be funded which might otherwise face problems, to allow management to obtain a larger equity stake than they otherwise might have expected, and to provide equity investors with a greater return through increased leverage. The trend in mezzanine in deals for a transaction price of at least £10m. is shown in Table 1.6.

Mezzanine debt is not confined to large buy-out transactions but is also used in those deals below a total purchase price of £10m. In the period 1985 to June 1989, CMBOR identified thirty-eight buy-outs with a total of £28.1m. of mezzanine debt at this smaller end of the market. An example is the Basis Loan Instrument used by Barclays Development Capital in some of its deals. Despite this growth, few institutions were undertaking large numbers of deals involving mezzanine.

Specialist mezzanine funds in the United Kingdom were raised in 1988/9 in the form of First Britannia Mezzanine and Intermediate Capital Group, both for £200m. Standard Chartered Bank and GE Capital Corporate Finance also announced substantial availability of mezzanine finance and Kleinwort Benson established a fund for both UK and European buy-outs.

Deferred payments have been a feature of buy-outs for many years, but of themselves involve limited vendor participation in the financing of the deal. The retention of vendor equity stakes through the investment of sale proceeds in shares in Newco, and vendor notes or the provision of loans on favourable terms have been significant features of some large UK buy-outs such as MFI, Reedpack and Bricom. These arrangements help bridge financing gaps and also enable vendors to share in future capital gains.

Table 1.6 UK mezzanine buy-outs/buy-ins
of £10m. or more

Year	Number	Value mezzanine (£m.)	Total value mezzanine deals (£m.)	Mezzanine total/ total value (%)
1985	5	92.4	420.6	22.0
1986	10	104.2	503.2	20.7
1987	15	239.3	1,604.4	14.9
1988*	20	172.0	1,220.8	14.1
1989Q2	17	187.5	1,358.1	13.8

* Excludes BPCC completed in January 1989 with a £40m. mezzanine layer.

Source: CMBOR.

The growth of various debt instruments has been closely linked to the completion of larger deals in the United Kingdom with strong and stable cash flow. Instruments, such as interest rate caps and collars are available to deal with some of the effects of interest-rate uncertainty. However, the significant rise in interest rates in the United Kingdom in 1989 and its effects on economic activity raised the general issue of the vulnerability of highly leveraged buy-out structures. Buy-outs in some parts of the retail sector, which have been buoyant for some time, may be particularly vulnerable to downturns in retail spending resulting from the higher cost of consumer credit. Hence in mid-1989 notable buy-outs such as MFI and Magnet, and buy-ins such as Lowndes Queensway became the subject of concern. MFI and Lowndes Queensway experienced difficulties in meeting finance servicing targets and had to seek restructuring. Magnet was faced by an inability to syndicate debt as lenders grew concerned at the difficulties of the retail sector. The Isosceles buy-in of the Gateway supermarket group also had difficulty in syndicating all the debt finance.

The European Dimension

Buy-outs and buy-ins in continental Europe have lagged considerably behind those in the United Kingdom and the United States. However from 1988 onwards there has been rapid development in several countries. The different levels of activity seen in continental European countries reflect the varying extent to which the necessary conditions for the development of a buy-out market apply. As for the United Kingdom, these concern the willingness of managers to become owners and the existence or development of an entrepreneurial culture; the industrial structure of a country and the existing willingness to change ownership as influenced by merger activity and the need to deal with retirement problems in family-owned firms; the presence of adequate and appropriate financing by banks and venture capital firms; the types of and roles played by intermediaries; the legal and taxation framework; and the size, status and development of stock markets, especially secondary tiers.

Up to the end of 1987, significant buy-out and buy-in activity had been recorded in Ireland, the Netherlands, Sweden and France (Table 1.7), although the sources of such deals were quite different. In Ireland, 73 per cent were divestments, a third of which were sales by foreign firms wishing to exit the country, a further 22 per

Table 1.7 Estimates of buy-outs and
buy-ins in Europe to the end of 1989

Country	1980–1987	1988	1989
Austria	5	5	5
Belgium	30	10	12
Denmark	12	20	31
Finland	10	14	16
France	200	100	130
W. Germany	50	36	25
Ireland	105	14	12
Italy	22	10	21
Netherlands	174	30	41
Norway	13	8	8
Spain	10–15	8	12
Sweden	18	22	32
Switzerland	10–20	5	21
UK	2,006	482	504

Source: CMBOR

cent were receivership cases, reflecting the country's economic problems, and only 5 per cent were retirement deals. The proximity to the United Kingdom in terms of the development of financial institutions and industrial cultures provided the basis for being able to complete buy-out deals. Both the Netherlands and Sweden were influenced significantly in the development of their buy-out markets by divestment by foreign-owned firms, with important influences on the ability to complete deals being the development of venture-capital markets well ahead of those in many other European countries and the willingness of banks to fund deals. In addition, the Netherlands had a legal and fiscal regime conducive to buy-outs and Sweden had a relatively active mergers and acquisitions market. The venture-capital and take-over markets in France have developed rapidly in recent years with a relaxation of the importance of the role of the state in industry and a desire by French industry to position itself to take advantage of international developments. Most importantly from a buy-out viewpoint, the succession problem faced by many thousands of French family-held businesses led to the introduction of an advantageous tax regime in 1984, subsequently modified in 1987, specifically aimed at stimulating buy-outs as a means of dealing with this issue. The introduction of fiscal consolidation generally in early 1988, means that many of the provisions of the specific buy-out legislation are now superseded. As a result, there has been a parallel growth in larger deals where management hold a minority of the equity and which now obtain the benefits of fiscal consolidation but would not have qualified under the original regime. In France, about 73 per cent of buy-outs are of family firms with approximately 23 per cent being divestments, and 2.5 per cent each being stock market firms (see below) and privatisation from the state sector (although with the return of the socialist government in 1988 this source has been sharply reduced). The development of expertise in such domestic institutions as Banexi, Initiative et Finance, Avenir Entreprise and LBO France, as well as French offices of foreign-owned institutions like 3i, Charterhouse and Citicorp, and foreign participation in funds (e.g., Ciclad and the Schroder and Dillon Read French funds) and directly in deals (e.g. Prudential Venture Managers in Cotes Desfossés) means that larger and syndicated deals are being completed. In 1988 the largest ten deals were completed for a total purchase price of Fr.f.13.8bn. Although vendor resistance to sale to unknown outside individuals is only slowly diminishing, buy-ins are also being completed such as Meccano, Cotes Desfossés and Pier Import (part buy-out/part buy-in). In family businesses with inadequate incumbent management teams the buy-in may be an important means by which independence may be maintained.

The close relationship between banks and firms, and the existence of a management cadre which was traditional, highly remunerated and unwilling to take risks, have been important elements which have slowed the development of a buy-out market in West Germany. Until the late 1980s, too, the venture-capital market and second and regional stock markets were underdeveloped. There was also less pressure to sell family-owned firms, especially outside the local community or through the banks. However, the need to solve succession problems in a growing number of family businesses at a time when cross-border activity has increased due to the positioning of firms in advance of the single European market in 1992, coupled with a growing appreciation of the phenomenon, has led to noticeable growth in the West German buy-out market. Indeed, as the market begins to open up it is becoming clearer that the extent of previous activity, which was surrounded in secrecy, is greater than earlier estimates have suggested. A stimulus came in 1988/9 through proposed changes in the tax regime which would have reduced the incentive to sell family businesses, bringing forward some buy-outs ahead of the date they were due to become effective. Although amendments to the proposed changes have now reduced the incentive to sell early, it nevertheless appears that an important stimulus to the development of the market has occurred. A feature of such deals is that founders have cashed out part of their holding, retaining an interest in the firm.

Elsewhere in continental Europe, buy-out activity has been relatively small, partly due to the size of some economies and partly to the absence of appropriate conditions. As the political situation changes in Eastern Europe, buy-outs are beginning to emerge as acceptable options in economic restructuring. At the time of writing, only Hungary has seen a deal completed, but buy-outs are known to be under active discussion in Poland and Yugoslavia. In those Western European countries with hitherto relatively little activity it was clear that in 1988/9 the markets were showing signs of significant growth, including the completion of a small number of large and stock-market deals. Indeed, two marked general features of the development of the surge in the buy-out market throughout continental Europe in 1988/9 were the appearance of very large deals (defined here as those completed for a total purchase price of at least £25m.) and of stock-market transactions (Table 1.8).

The annual number of large deals in all continental Europe countries taken together remains well below that seen in the United Kingdom alone. Some of these are stock-market deals, to which we return shortly, but others are buy-outs of large family firms and divestments from foreign-owned parents. Even some large stock-market deals are essentially exits by original family shareholders.

Large divestments were seen in 1988 in France (Saunier Duval from Saint Gobain; Fruehauf Europe from Fruehauf Inc.), Italy

Table 1.8 European buy-outs and buy-ins:
1989 over-£25m. deals* and stock market transactions

	No. of deals over £25m.	No. of stock-market deals[‡]	Largest deal in 1989
UK	32[†]	9	£631m.[†]
France	10	9	FFr.1.3bn.
Italy	5	0	over L100bn.
Sweden	3	3	Skr.3,930m.
Spain	0	0	confidential
Netherlands	1	0	HFl 170m.
Belgium	0	0	BFr.1,300m.
W. Germany	4	0	DM540m.
Switzerland	4	0	SFr.60m.
Denmark	1	1	Dkr805m.

* As recorded on CMBOR database.
[†] Buy-outs only.
[‡] Figures may include deals under £25m.
Source: CMBOR.

(Fata European Group from FKI-Babcock, Rimoldi from Rockwell Inc.), Switzerland (Juvena from Beecham), the Netherlands (IMS Overseas from International Mill Services Inc.), Belgium (C and F Holdings from Centrafarm Group NV) and Luxembourg (Bay State Abrasives from its US parent). It is interesting to note the preponderance amongst these large divestments of foreign vendors. It should also be noted that the Fruehauf buy-out, though based in France, was a transnational buy-out of the whole European operation of the US parent. Transnational or cross-border buy-outs, though potentially posing complex structuring issues, offer a means by which a non-European vendor can exit from all its European operations in one deal. Where they involve UK or US vendors they may also be a means by which financing institutions and advisers in these countries can make use of their lead in expertise to gain significant market share. Large buy-outs of private family companies have been seen recently in France, Italy, Spain, Sweden and most notably Germany. The increasing frequency of German deals has already been noted, but the buy-outs of Sachtler, Heidemann in 1988 and Lignotock in 1989 demonstrate the feasibility of this type of transaction in dealing with succession issues in large private firms in Germany.

The extent of stock-market buy-outs in the United Kingdom has already been noted. It is interesting to record that France exceeded the United Kingdom for this kind of deal in 1988, with three stock-market buy-outs to mid-1989 (Latecoere, SIACO and Gérard Pasquier), eight in 1988 (Darty, SAMSE, Moulinex, Pier Import, Epeda-Bértrand Faure, Atelier Breton de Réparation Ferroviaire, Berger-Levrault and Normere) and a further five prior to 1988 (Sagem, Docks Industriels, Installux, SMT-Goupil and Guy Degrene). These deals have involved companies quoted on a range of stock markets from the Paris main market to provincial over-the-counter markets. A key feature has been the desire by family shareholders, who are often in the majority, to liquidate their holdings. Hence, in France such buy-outs are another manifestation of the succession problem in family firms. However, the deal may be a cash-out device, by which the share capital can be restructured leaving family shareholders with a significant minority stake. In Darty, the largest buy-out in France to date, family shareholders retain a fifth of the equity. Stock-market buy-outs to pre-empt, or as a defence against, a hostile take-over bid are now evident in France, and are an important means of retaining the independent existence of large previously family-controlled firms. SMT-Goupil and Pier Import, for example, were the subject of a buy-out and buy-in, respectively, in order to pre-empt a hostile take-over. The management of Epeda-Bértrand Faure were successful in their buy-out in the face of an unwelcome bid from Valeo, but in the case of Télémécanique, Schneider defeated a buy-out attempt. An important element in the Epeda-Bértrand Faure case was the support for the management bid, in preference to that by Valeo, by a friendly group of share-holders. Such groups of financial institutions and industrial firms are traditionally a central characteristic of the French take-over market.

Elsewhere in Europe, stock-market buy-outs are so far rare, reflecting the state of development of both the buy-out and stock markets. The A/S Plastmontage stock-market buy-out in Denmark involved a company where the founder was still the majority owner. Interestingly, management's equity stake is dependent upon a market mechanism. The Gunnebo buy-out in Sweden was enabled by the sale of an investment company's major share-holdings in the company and occurred after several years of restructuring by the incumbent management. However, at the end of 1989 there were several going private deals pending in Sweden, emphasising the developed nature of that country's buy-out market. The management of the Dutch quoted company Twijnstra Gudde acquired an initial majority stake in the firm, subsequently purchasing the remaining shares in 1988.

UK and US investors, such as 3i, Citicorp and Charterhouse, have based offices in continental Europe to undertake buy-outs there, whilst others have participated in deals either at arm's length or through the establishment of alliances with domestically based institutions in individual countries. As in the United Kingdom, development of the continental European buy-out market has been accompanied by the establishment of specialist buy-out funds, either wholly domestically based, or involving foreign investors, such as the Ciclad fund involving Candover, Barclays Development Capital and other institutions from the United Kingdom in partnership with domestic French investors.

Schroders have established specialist German, Italian and French funds, Dillon Read specialist French and Spanish ones, whilst Barings, Granville and Hambro have wider European trusts. The first specialist European buy-in fund has been established by MMG Patricof.

Buy-outs in the United States

The buy-out market in the United States has been established somewhat longer than is the case for the United Kingdom, and displays certain marked differences from experience so far on this side of the Atlantic. In particular, the role of outside deal-makers using substantial amounts of debt-funding to effect buy-outs has been considerably more important than in the United Kingdom. Recent developments in the United Kingdom, as noted earlier, such as some buy-in attempts at public companies, display characteristics of the US leveraged buy-out. In addition, the growth of buy-outs of stock-market companies also reflects a significant element of the US market.

Trends in the two main sectors of the US buy-out market, divestitures and going privates, are shown for the period 1979–1988 in Table 1.9. The number of buy-outs occurring on divestment peaked in 1986, with a sharp decline in 1987. In value terms, 1986 was also a peak, although known deal value recovered in 1988 to its second-highest-ever level. The average known size of deals is markedly above that for divestment buy-outs in the United Kingdom, although this figure is probably biased upwards as the larger deals are more likely to have their prices made known. In 1988, US divestment buy-outs accounted for one-tenth of all sales of subsidiaries by number, the lowest level since 1981 and well below the proportion seen in the United Kingdom.

By far the largest proportion of deal value is accounted for by going-private deals, which exceeded $60bn. in 1988 as a result of the RJR Nabisco buy-out. The numbers involved were well below those for divestments up to 1987. However, after falling sharply in 1987 going privates reached record levels in 1988 and for the first time exceeded divestment buy-outs. The reasons for this change are

Table 1.9 US buy-outs

Year	Total number	Divestment number with value	Value ($m.)	Source average ($m.)	Number	Going private value ($m.)	Average ($m.)
1979	59	14	47	3.3	16	636	39.8
1980	47	15	363	24.2	13	967	74.4
1981	83	30	484	16.1	17	2,339	137.6
1982	115	41	1,361	33.2	31	2,837	91.5
1983	139	51	2,499	49.0	36	7,145	198.5
1984	122	42	3,833	91.3	57	10,806	415.6
1985	132	50	5,005	100.1	76	24,140	317.6
1986	144	57	9,542	167.4	76	20,232	281.0
1987	90	43	5,857	138.5	47	22,057	469.3
1988	89	47	8,522	181.3	125	60,921	487.4

Source: Mergerstat Review, Merrill Lynch.

closely related to movements in stock-market indices in the last three years.

Going-private deals may involve management, who already hold a significant equity stake, buying out the company with substantial leverage. Alternatively, the initiative may come from an external group of individuals or a specialist buy-out firm, who organise the company and possibly include management in the equity. However, such deals may occur in direct competition with an incumbent management buy-out attempt, as in the case of RJR Nabisco, or may result in incumbent management being replaced by a new team, some members of which may be employees of the specialist buy-out institution. Going-private buy-outs have been the subject of considerable discussion in the United States and the issues which are raised are pertinent to the development of this kind of transaction in the United Kingdom. We return to this topic in Chapter 2.

Conclusions

The review of trends presented in this chapter has demonstrated how management buy-outs and buy-ins have become international phenomena. In the United Kingdom, the last three years have seen increased emphasis upon very large deals, although it is important not to forget that the actual number of smaller deals is currently at its highest level. The buy-in market has now become firmly established in the United Kingdom, with particularly important developments in respect of buy-ins of divested subsidiaries and of hostile buy-ins of publicly quoted companies appearing in 1989. The increased incidence of quoted company buy-outs and buy-ins brings UK experience closer to that seen in the United States, particularly with the appearance of unbundling and greater use of mezzanine finance. However, a quoted mezzanine debt market has yet to appear in the United Kingdom.

Continental European experience of buy-outs and buy-ins has developed rapidly from 1988 onwards, although the number and size of deals completed varies significantly from one country to another. Nevertheless, it is now clear that large transactions, including those involving quoted companies, are feasible. UK and US institutions have also established a significant market presence in several continental European countries. The rationale for buying-out is examined in the next chapter.

CHAPTER 2

Why buy-out?

As we have seen in Chapter 1, the buy-out market-place has developed rapidly over the last decade. Although this growth means that many owners and managers have asked themselves the question 'why buy-out?' and have found convincing answers, nevertheless there remain many for whom management buy-outs have not been adopted as a tool of strategy. Our aim in this chapter is to explain the circumstances in which buying-out may prove attractive. Given developments in the legal and financial framework surrounding buy-outs the discussion should be of interest both to those who have experienced buy-outs and those who have not. In the former case, these developments open up new buy-out opportunities which may not have been possible in the first wave of the phenomenon.

Buying-out, in common with any transaction, requires the existence of a willing seller and a willing purchaser; as a consequence discussion of why a buy-out may be appropriate needs to be viewed from two perspectives. As the perspectives of the vendor and the puchaser may be quite different this will affect whether or not a buy-out takes place and the form it takes. It is against this background that the sources of buy-out, categorised as in Figure 2.1, are discussed. Essentially buy-outs may take place from either parts of parent companies or through the purchase of an entire independent company. From these broad categories a number of sub-categories may be discerned, which are addressed in turn.

Buy-outs from Parent Firms

In this section we shall first of all examine how the opportunity for a buy-out may arise as part of a parent firm's review of competitive strategy and then go on to consider how a parent company may need to take action to prevent a buy-out taking place where it is deemed unhelpful to the parent's future direction. For ease of presentation attention will mainly be focused upon that part of Figure 2.1 which shows a buy-out occurring on a divestment where no trading relationship exists with the parent. At the end of the section, attention is drawn to the other possibilities for buy-outs from parents.

Buy-outs and Corporate Strategy

Elements of corporate strategy include decisions on diversification, investment, acquisition and divestment. However, there has been a tendency in the past for the process of divestment to be regarded in an unfavourable light, either through a bias towards the acquisitive side of any transaction, or through a belief that divestment was the result of some past error, or was a sign of defeat of some kind. This has done the process a great disservice. In any diverse corporate entity growth and realignment through acquisition and divestment should be natural considerations for corporate strategists. Choices have to be made about the shape and direction of any corporate body. Where a currently owned subsidiary does not fit in with the perceived future strategy, it is natural to wish to sell. Indeed, a sale may be necessary in order to raise cash to effect a desired change of course. We can thus consider divestment as detailed in Table 2.1 as arising out of the strategic review forming part of a programme of ordered change, or as a result of some corporate crisis to which a solution must be found. In either case there will be factors which act to promote the divestment route and those which act to inhibit it. In any process of considered realignment it would be opportune to sell when in the corporate view the subsidiary's value is at a maximum, where it no longer fits the desired mix of activities, or where it is an ill-fitting element which was only acquired as part of a package which contained parts the company wanted – the 'string bag effect'. However, inertia, a desire to absorb and reorganise rather than sell and the constraints which the market may impose at any particular time may act to inhibit the process. In crisis the divestment route is

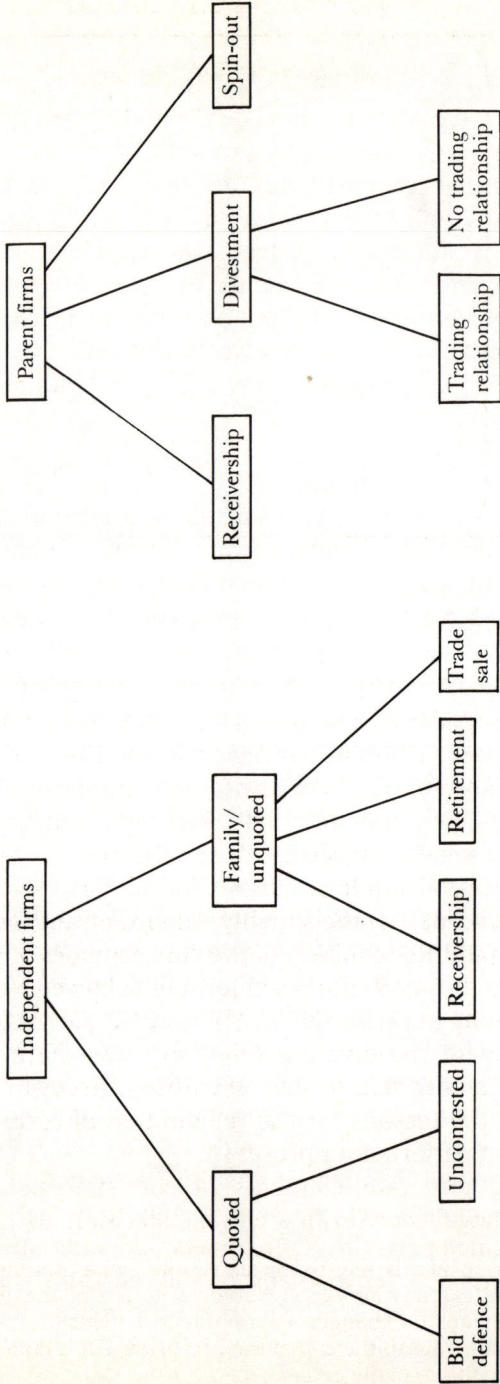

Figure 2.1 Buy-out sources

Table 2.1 Factors affecting divestment

Strategic change	Ordered change	Promoters Value at maximum Change of corporate direction 'String bag effect' Inhibitors Inertia Absorption/reorganisation Market constraints
	Crisis	Promoters Cash flow Cost base rationalisation Loss elimination Inhibitors Saleability (lack of) Logic link Strategic importance

often required as a result of problems of liquidity, uncompetitiveness, and unprofitability. However, a sale may not be possible or feasible as the subsidiary may be unsellable, there may be a logical link with other integrated processes, or it may be necessary to maintain a strategic presence in a particular sector to defend existing interests.

A survey by CMBOR carried out in 1987 of all buy-outs completed between mid-1983 and the first quarter of 1986 which produced 182 respondent firms asked for a ranking of the main reasons that vendors wished to sell (Table 2.2).[*] Managers were asked to score the vendor's reasons for sale on a scale from one to seven, where one signified highly important and seven indicated low importance. Redefinition of the core activities of the group was easily the most important reason for sale, followed by various other reasons relating to performance. For non-UK parents, future capital requirements of the divested subsidiary was the most important element in the decision to sell. Of course it needs to be recognised that one of the reasons for the redefinition of core activities may relate to poor performance prospects.

Once the disparate elements of the strategic value of the subsidiary have been evaluated, the decision to divest may be

---

[*] This survey, which is referred to at various points throughout the book, updates and extends an earlier survey reported in the first edition. The survey picks up the changed environment in which buy-outs took place from the mid-1980s to the end of the decade, which is in marked contrast to the crisis conditions of the earlier period.

Table 2.2 Divestors' reasons for selling

	Divestor		
	UK parent	Non-UK parent	All sellers by buy-out
Liquidation	5.78	7.00	4.26
Lack of profitability	3.00	3.10	3.04
Cash-flow problems	3.35	4.33	3.54
Poor growth prospects	3.48	3.89	3.67
Re-definition of core activities of group	2.06	2.12	2.31

Note: Scores are survey averages on a range from 1 to 7 where 1 = most important and 7 = least important.

Source: CMBOR survey of buy-outs between mid-1983 and the first quarter of 1986.

taken. It is then necessary to consider what form the divestment should take, and it is at this stage that the role of the buy-out may be examined and the advantages and disadvantages of this form of ownership transfer considered for any particular divestment. Essentially the issue reduces to sale to management versus sale to an external purchaser. Simply stated, sale to management takes place because it offers the parent company the most attractive transaction overall. However, identifying the precise conditions under which this occurs is less straightforward.

In determining what constitutes the preferred outcome for the vendor it is necessary to examine not simply the financial position but also the whole panoply of other considerations which, though they may have financial implications, are likely to be more difficult to quantify precisely. Besides wanting the best price, the management of the parent may have preferences about how the price is to be paid, how (or if) the deal is to be made public, the speed at which the transaction is completed, its reputation in the locality in which the subsidiary is located and the wider reputation of the company in the market-place. Much will depend upon how the decision to sell was arrived at in the first place and whether the sale is contested or not. If the sale is contested, that is to say if there is an external purchaser (or a number of external purchasers) with whom the internal management have to compete, the price of the subsidiary will be tested in the market-place. In an uncontested transfer, the price will simply be a matter for negotiation between the vendor and the management effecting the purchase. In the latter case the parent has no immediate guide to the true market value of the subsidiary if the bid is not made public. If publicity does not bring forth a counter bid when the general price is known then they may be satisfied that there is no higher-value deal on offer.

However, where all is kept secret the parent will not really know the price that has been paid for secrecy! Whether the bid is contested is very much in the hands of the vendor. If there is a competition for the subsidiary in which the incumbent management are bidding then the pattern of events becomes important. It matters whether it was an outside bid which prompted management to offer a counter, or whether it occurred the other way round. There is certainly great merit from the vendor's point of view in the general case for ensuring that the internal management will have their offer tested against that of an outside bidder.

How the potential sale may arise in line with the individual parties' strategies is outlined in Table 2.3 and it is worth expanding on these points. The figure outlines whether the transaction is seen by each of the parties to be for defensive, neutral or offensive reasons. In other words, is the divestment by the parent, for example, forced on it as a defence to some external threat, is it simply part of some ongoing process of change or is it part of an offensive strategy to shift the nature and direction of the business? Each of the boxes in Table 2.3 can be expanded in turn.

The factors which may force the parent on the defensive include a cash crisis, and this position can lead to two types of sale of subsidiary. Either the parent sells the subsidiary which is the cause of the financial problem, and thus moves back towards health by removing the cash haemorrhage, or it is forced to sell that which is most immediately saleable in order to generate cash to satisfy creditors. In the former case it is the bad parts of the business that are on offer but in the latter it is often the best. The management in the subsidiaries should be in a position to know the specific contribution that their area is making to the corporate whole, and

Table 2.3 Strategic considerations on sale/purchase evaluation

	Defensive	Neutral	Offensive
Parent	Need to protect overall entity	Unwanted assets post strategic review	Strategic shift in corporate directions
Subsidiary management	Threat to position	Unexpected opportunity to buy	Knowledge of unrealised potential
External bidder	Protect existing interests	Intermediary approach/ unexpected catalyst	Strategic opportunity

are thus in a position to take maximum advantage of an opportunity. The neutral reasons may include part of the natural process of evolution and the 'string bag effect'. The parent may take the initiative in going on the offensive by actively seeking to sell the subsidiary as part of a major shift of direction and may approach the incumbent management about purchase. It is also possible that the parent may have to defend itself from an unwelcome bid for a subsidiary which comes from inside, and this vital strategic issue will be discussed shortly.

The management team in a subsidiary may see the buy-out as a defence against the unwelcome attentions of an outside bid which places their position in jeopardy. The buy-out may also occur as a result of an unexpected opportunity to buy. The management team may, however, mount an offensive strategy and actively seek to buy out their subsidiary in circumstances where they are confident that the current value to the parent understates its true value. The opportunity for personal gain in this situation is present and prompts the question of moral hazard which will be returned to later.

In the case of an external purchaser it is possible to see the motives in the same terms. The proposed acquisition may be to protect existing interests, for example through the purchase of excess capacity in an industry; as the result of some approach by an intermediary which only then places the target in the bidder's mind, or as part of a strategic offensive to acquire a company offering a strategic fit with existing activities, or permitting entry to a new market or enabling a position of market dominance to be obtained.

The decision to sell to management will require that, after consideration of all the strategic factors, the deal offers the best possible return for the vendor who has responsibilities to the shareholders to ensure that the overall terms of the sale are the most attractive. Essentially the issue will revolve around the respective valuations which the parties place on any subsidiary. Some of the key factors which will affect this valuation are detailed in Table 2.4

Valuation is a subjective matter and it is the decision-maker's perception of events that is important in determining the value which is placed upon any commercial opportunity. The directions indicated in Table 2.4 are only suggestive, and the effects of some events may be somewhat ambiguous. From examination of the figures it may be discerned that the local management would be in a strong position (i.e. likely to be able to buy the subsidiary as they

Table 2.4 Factors affecting relative valuation of a subsidiary for sale

		Valuation by		
		Management of parent	Management of external bidder	Management of subsidiary
Risk preference of parties	Risk preference	↓	↓	↑
	Risk avoidance	↑	↑	↓
Shareholder control of parent	High	↑	↓	n/a
	Low	↓	↑	n/a
Performance effect of sale on overall group	Improve	↓	↑	n/a
	Fall	↑	↓	n/a
Performance effect of sale on subsidiary sold	Improve	n/a	↑	↑
	Fall	n/a	↓	↓
Effect of sale on local reputation	Harmed	↑	↓	↑
	Improved	↓	↑	↓
Speed of sale required by vendor	Quick	↓	↓	↓
	Slow	↑	↑	↑
Management contribution to subsidiary	High	↓ *	↓ *	↑
	Low	↑ *	↑ *	↓
Financeability of sale	Easy	n/a	↑	↑
	Difficult	n/a	↓	↓
Strategy of parent	Offensive	↑	↑	↓
	Defensive	↓	↓	↑
Subsidiary management control of information	High	↓	↓	↑
	Low	↑	↑	↓

* Assumes management do not stay with subsidiary on sale, or sale causes dissatisfaction.
Note: Arrows indicate direction of effect on valuation for each party.

value it more highly than the external bidder) where they are more amenable to taking the risk involved in the purchase (though their insider knowledge would make it less of a risk to them than to an external purchaser), where a significant local reputation exists, where the local management is an important part of the value of the company, and where local management has significant control over the flow of information within the company. These factors are not uncommon and can explain many of the buy-outs that have been observed in the United Kingdom. When taken together with the specific strategic needs of the parents, in many instances they contrived to produce sales at less than book value in the early wave of buy-outs. Discounts may still arise in, for example, heavy industrial companies with low return on capital and negligible or indeed negative profits. However, relative to the general mix of buy-outs there are few of these transactions compared to the early 1980s, with many buy-outs involving significant goodwill elements.

Internal Management Issues or When to Say 'No'

Once the buy-out has become established as an alternative means by which a parent company may divest itself of an unwanted subsidiary, and whilst such widespread publicity is given to the spectacular successes which can arise from such sales, there must be an effect on the performance, aims and aspirations of many management teams within large conglomerate groups. A desire to buy out may be kindled where it did not exist before, and an established desire may be promoted more soundly through the existence of models to follow. These aspects may be difficult to deal with for the management of a parent group and add a dimension to the internal management of firms that did not exist before. The issues of asymmetry of information and insider knowledge take on added significance for the parent that is unwilling to sell a subsidiary. They may even constitute an enemy within! Traditional ideas of management development, promotion and hierarchical aspirations within a group or individual managers leaving a position for a more attractive one elsewhere may be replaced by whole teams seeking to take away a bundle of assets in the form of a new independent company. This concept has several implications.

The conglomerate parent will have to examine very carefully the structure of rewards and incentives which exist within the group. There is clear evidence from our research that the buy-out teams are motivated by a desire for independence in decision-making, a desire to 'run their own show' and to reap the rewards in terms of significant changes in their personal wealth. In the CMBOR survey of buy-outs completed between mid-1983 and early 1986, managers were asked to score their reasons for buying out on a scale from one to seven, where one signified high importance and seven indicated low importance. The positive factors relating to desires to control one's own business and long-term faith in the company showed most strongly, with negative factors to do with fears of redundancy, and of new owners, being least important. Lack of head-office restraints was placed fourth in order of importance (Table 2.5).

The encouragement of independence and entrepreneurship within a group may have significant benefits for the company wishing to keep its management teams intact where they are linked to holdings of equity in the company which offer the prospect of a

Table 2.5 Managers' reasons for buying-out

	Buy-outs from		
	UK parent	Non-UK parent	All buy-outs
Control own business	2.07	2.09	2.01
Lack of head-office restraints	3.62	3.81	3.85
Better financial rewards	3.07	2.76	2.98
Fear of redundancy	5.21	5.38	5.20
Fear of new owner	5.68	5.00	5.28
Long-term faith in company	2.55	2.09	2.55
To develop own talents	3.70	4.15	3.53

Note: scores are defined as in Table 2.2.

Source: CMBOR.

capital gain. Moreover, it may also help to avoid the possibility of knock-on effects in other subsidiaries were a buy-out to take place in one of them. (This is a major reason for much of the secrecy surrounding buy-outs; parent company boards may not wish to encourage others to do the same.)

The phenomenon also emphasises the need for close central control of information flows and tests of its reliability. If the advantage of insider knowledge on the part of the management of subsidiary companies does *not* exist then it increases the probability that should a sale take place, it will fully reflect the present value of the part, with true future potential included. Caution must always be exercised to ensure that the managements of subsidiaries are indeed managing the interests of the group and not acting in such a way as to make a buy-out probable, or preparing the ground at the parent's expense for a buy-out which has already been intimated. There is a significant problem of moral hazard for the management of subsidiaries to face. Where does their true personal interest lie? But what are their legal and moral obligations to the owners in their current employment? When do they declare an interest? How do they perform during the transitional phase? What can their position be if the buy-out does not proceed? The existence of opportunities and desires to buy out, if spread widely, can fundamentally change the relationships at senior levels within companies. Whilst they have the potential to be useful avenues for corporate adaptation they can also generate internal uncertainties to which attention should be given.

One way in which an unwilling parent may defend itself against the unwelcome buy-out is to ensure that the subsidiary management teams are never in a position to buy-out. This could be achieved by keeping close central control so that the independence and completeness of local management never exists, or by keeping key executives on the move within a group so that teams never form. Both are extremely dangerous and potentially damaging to the group where centralisation may be ineffective and inappropriate, and mobility uneconomic and wasteful of expertise. Given the propensity for buy-outs to be initiated by 'key' figures, the policy of mobility may also give individuals too much knowledge of the whole operation. It is certain that if a parent has had to fight off an unwelcome buy-out attempt there can never be a return to the status quo ante. The fundamental change in the relationships from one of superior–subordinate to one of buyer–seller during the negotiation will seldom be susceptible to repair. Indeed it may well be expected that the team will resign if the bid is a failure and that in itself can prove very costly to the parent. If the potential buy-out team had not had ability then they would not have tried to buy out, and certainly would not have been able to get financial support. Despite this, in some cases of unwanted buy-out bids, management have been dismissed rather than being allowed to resign.

Other Buy-outs from Parent Groups
Chapter 1 showed that most buy-outs arise on divestment of subsidiaries or divisions from larger groups. In such cases, the buy-out involved is generally a non-core activity with no trading relationship with its former parent. However, there is a significant number of instances where trading activity takes place both before and after the transfer of ownership (see Table 2.6). This trading may involve the parent as a supplier (about 25 per cent of cases) or, more noticeably as a customer (about 40 per cent of cases). The relationship may take the form of the provision of a service, such as computer systems, or as an input to a production process. In the majority of cases, parental trading accounted for less than 10 per cent of the buy-outs' sales or purchases, although for about 7 per cent of buy-outs, the parent accounted for at least 20 per cent of sales. Sale to management where a trading relationship exists may be an attractive option for the parent. In these cases parent companies may take a more pro-active view in agreeing to a buy-out, so that by taking the initiative rather than waiting to be forced into a deal, the parent may put itself into a strong position to establish terms and conditions. Such an approach has already been used in a few cases to enable parents to improve the efficiency and lower the cost of their supplies. The move may be attractive where

Table 2.6 Trading between buy-out and former parent

	Survey of buy-outs completed			
	Pre-mid-1983		Mid-1983–early 1986	
	Number	%	Number	%
1. Parent as customer				
Yes	27	39.7	51	39.3
No	41	60.3	79	60.7
	68	100.0	130	100.0
2. Parent as supplier				
Yes	16	23.5	35	27.0
No	52	76.5	95	73.0
	68	100.0	130	100.0

Sources:
1. Pre-mid 1983: M.Wright and J. Coyne, *Management Buy-outs*, Croom-Helm, Beckenham, 1985.
2. CMBOR survey of buy-outs between mid-1983 and the first quarter of 1986.

the parent has alternative suppliers outside the group already and where the subsidiary supplies a significant portion of its output to the parent. By sale to management the parent can use the implied threat of using other external suppliers as one means of encouraging efficient supply. The other essential feature is that by becoming owners, managers have the incentive to perform efficiently whereas previously this was not the case, nor was the parent able to enforce a high level of efficiency. In cases where trading relationships exist, parents may wish to retain a minority equity stake, both to enable the deal to be completed and also to maintain subsequent influence.

A rather more specialist kind of buy-out where trading relationships exist arose following the Lloyd's Act of 1982 which prevented broking groups from continuing to own a managed agency business after 1987. In September 1985 the management, in the form of Wellington Underwriting Agencies, acquired the managing agency business of Willis Faber and Dumas (Agencies), and there have been many similar instances. Similarly the break-up of National Bus, referred to in more detail below, involved divestment outside the control of the group itself.

A significant number of receivership buy-outs are of subsidiaries or divisions of groups. Hence, in this extreme form of corporate crisis, groups which are not viable as a whole may contain within themselves parts which have the potential to be successful on their own. Two notable buy-outs of this type have been Stone

International and Mansfield Shoe (1981). Stone International was a buy-out from the liquidation of Stone-Platt in May 1982. The company was acquired by the management and re-acquired a full stock-market listing in October 1984. After flotation it undertook significant acquisition activity and in the process of integrating these new activities into the group sold certain unwanted parts to their management, hence creating what might be termed second-generation buy-outs. However, the company's fortunes subsequently declined dramatically and it was taken over. Mansfield Shoe (1981) was a buy-out from the collapsed Norvic Securities. Since the buy-out took place, several other companies in receivership have been acquired, one of which was another shoe-producer. These businesses have themselves been turned round and now make a positive cash contribution to the original buy-out, which also repaid its external financing some years ahead of schedule. As we shall see in more detail later, two of the key reasons for success in these buy-outs in very different market areas were the ability to gain control over their own finances which previously had been drained away and the freedom to undertake actions in response to market opportunities which previously had been restricted.

These two buy-outs took place in the depths of a serious recession. For receivers and liquidators seeking to obtain the best return for creditors, such buy-outs may be attractive as a higher price may be placed on an entity sold as a going concern rather than a collection of assets. Management may be forced into purchasing some parts they did not particularly want, but may still obtain their company at a substantial discount to the price it would have had to pay if a buy-out had been attempted before the group's demise. Whilst it is always likely that groups will fail, this type of buy-out in periods of less severe contraction is less common as seen in the buy-out experience of the late 1980s.

The other major remaining element of buy-outs from parent groups is the spin-out. Until recently these were unheard of in the United Kingdom, though they have been a familiar part of the US industrial scene for a number of years. Termed 'spin-offs' in the United States, this type of transaction essentially involves the sale to management of a new, probably high-tech, venture which the managers themselves have been responsible for developing. The parent group retains an equity interest so as to obtain a share of future profits. The management, in becoming owners, gain the incentive in a more entrepreneurial environment to exploit fully the development, which may not have been possible under a group structure. Another example of a parent group acting pro-actively towards buy-outs is thus observed, since if a spin-off was not offered, the management may well have set up on their own anyway. This is a real possibility where the worth of a division is very much embodied in the skills of its employees. In an attempt to develop this phenomenon in the United Kingdom, 3i Ventures has promoted the sponsored spin-out, whereby a financing institution participates with management and the parent in funding the deal. Although it has been held that few spin-outs have occurred in the United Kingdom because of a lack of willingness on the part of management to venture out from under the protective corporate umbrella, this is hardly credible given the growth in management buy-out activity. More likely explanations concern the possible lack of the full range of managerial skills (especially finance) in R & D divisions, which calls into question their practical ability to survive independently, and a lack of appreciation of this type of joint venture on the part of group management.

Buy-outs from Independent Firms

As seen in Chapter 1, buy-outs of independent companies on the retirement of the owners reached record levels in 1988/89, with a further small number also occurring following the receivership of an independent company. While the latter have received a great deal of attention, not least because of their job-saving aspects, the former have tended to be by-passed despite the significant size of many of them. These companies may be sub-divided into family- and non-family-owned. In the former case ownership may be said to lie within the hands of members of the same family, though senior management may have a minority equity stake. Family ownership can extend from the founder, at one extreme, to siblings, cousins and more distant relations at the other. The first case may be referred to as first-generation family businesses and the second as concerning subsequent generations. This difference raises important issues, as will be seen shortly. Non-family-owned businesses may be distinguished from family firms by a spread of ownership between a number of individuals who are not members of the same family. Additionally since 1985, there have been buy-outs in the United Kingdom of quoted independent companies, something which has been a common feature of the US acquisition scene.

Buy-outs of Unquoted Companies

Essentially, three issues present themselves in the succession of a family firm: the development of the business by the founder, succession from the founder, and subsequent control of the firm. What happens in each of these three cases has implications for the feasibility of a management buy-out. Schematically, such a life-cycle approach to family businesses may be viewed as in Figure 2.2

Initially, the founder develops a good idea and with energy builds a fairly successful company. However, the very determination needed to produce a result can produce serious problems. Most notably, founders often refuse to delegate authority. Delegation may not be a problem in a relatively small company where the owner-manager is not approaching retirement. In larger companies, it may be physically impossible for the owner to keep adequate control of all aspects. Where the owner is nearing retirement, serious question marks are raised about the company's continuing existence. Either no adequate management hierarchy has been developed since the founder wants no challenge to his position to arise, or the natural family successors may have been prevented from gaining experience to run the business. In both these instances problems are in store if the founder, say, refuses to make changes necessary to cope with a new environment or indulges in excessive philanthropy towards employees. Other shareholders, even if they exist, are unlikely to have the voting

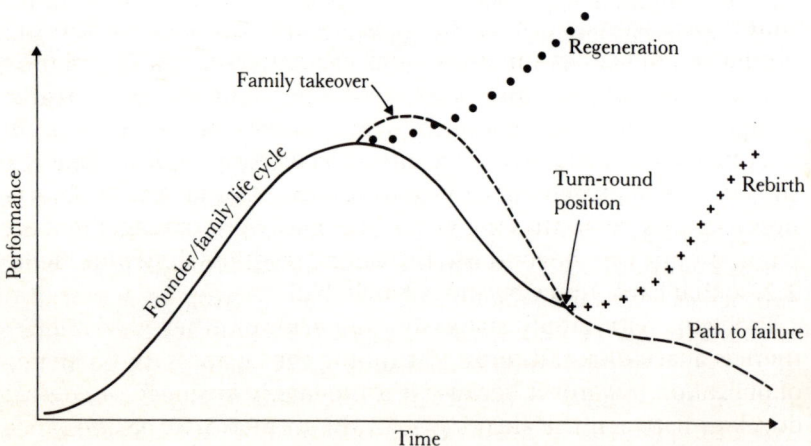

Figure 2.2   Family business and management buy-out life cycle

power to effect a change. The near disaster that may arise in such circumstances has been well documented in a spectacular vein in respect of the early days of the Ford Motor Company.

Of course, such is not always the case and a management buy-out opportunity may present itself on the retirement of the founder where no suitable family successor exists. In some cases, the founder may decide to hand on the business to the employees as a whole in the form of a Trust. Such conversion co-operatives have been an interesting parallel phenomenon to the management buy-out in recent years. The case of Baxi-Heating is perhaps one of the notable examples of this type of succession.

An appropriate strategy for a founder with no family successor may be to introduce new management into the firm some time ahead of planned retirement. The advantages here are that new management can familiarise themselves with the business and, if they buy an equity stake, have an incentive to see that the company performs well. A management buy-in at this stage as a prelude to a buy-out may be preferable to a buy-in at the time of the founder's retirement.

Family succession on the founder's retirement may help regenerate the business where the successor is competent and has been allowed to participate in decision-making. However, where this is not the case, the heir may attempt to show independence, with disastrous consequences. Typically, such action takes the form of trying to lead the company into new market areas, for which it is ill-equipped. The succession of the son of the founder of A and H Upholstery resulted in a shift away from production of three-piece suites for the medium to top end of the UK market towards production of leather suites for a European market. This move from a reasonable market niche exposed the company to a highly competitive environment with which it was not able to cope. Eventually the company went into receivership and became the subject of a management buy-out. Notions of pride and stubbornness can thus mean that the views of experienced management are ignored until way beyond the turnround position shown in Figure 2.2, so that bankruptcy becomes inevitable.

Problems with family successors can arise in other ways. Either there is a lack of real interest in running the business, but a feeling of obligation towards it because it is the family business, or conflict develops between the successors. In the former case, performance in the business may slowly decline without check. While adequate management may exist, it is prevented from taking appropriate action. The basis for a management buy-out may also exist, but both management and a potential financier or adviser are faced with a very delicate task of persuading family owners to let go. The family may find it advantageous to allow management to buy in a minority equity stake, with the possibility of staging a buy-out at some future time.

Where more than one successor exists, the conflicts which may be apparent in family relationships may become exacerbated in running the firm. Jealousies between siblings may lead them to charge each other with not pulling their weight, and may be emphasised where one feels the victim of a parent's favouritism for the other. Cousin–cousin conflicts show how these problems can carry through to subsequent generations. An inability to resolve these conflicts, for example, by introducing management to run the business, may mean that, short of receivership, sale of the business is the only way out. If a buy-out is to be a possibility, management need to be neutral between the rival family factions. Alternatively, sale to another group may be sought. A buy-out opportunity may present itself at some other date when the new parent needs to divest. At this point one or other side of the family may have the chance to buy back the family business. Given the extent of acquisition activity involving family firms since the 1960s, and the frequent retention of family members' managerial positions, there are undoubtedly a large number of potential buy-outs from this source yet to be realised. The buy-out of Timpson Shoes in late 1983 is typical of many cases of this source of ownership change. Developed originally as a family firm, the company was acquired in the early 1970s by UDS following irreconcilable differences between two parts of the family. The opportunity to buy out was presented shortly after the acquisition of UDS, which by this time had run into difficulties, by Hanson Trust. The buy-out, at a price of some £40m., was at the time the largest in the United Kingdom and was led by John Timpson, son of the chairman at the time of the acquisition, who had been the company's managing director during the period it was a subsidiary of UDS.

Buy-outs on the retirement of the previous owners have generally tended to be smaller than buy-outs from other sources. The CMBOR 1983/6 survey found average employment size prior to buy-out to be 130 employees in respect of retirement buy-outs, compared to an overall average of 252 employees. It is also interesting to record that buy-outs on retirement had the largest increases in employment between the period immediately before the buy-out and the time of the survey. In contrast, buy-outs of independent companies in receivership showed very significant falls, averaging almost two-fifths.

The succession issue in unquoted companies where ownership is spread between various families may be most easily solved by a trade sale. This may particularly be true where a split occurs between the shareholders such that neither willingly allows the other to acquire the company. Alternatively management may provide a suitable purchaser, though care is needed to ensure that they are not seen to be taking one side or the other in cases of a dispute.

Quoted Companies

Quoted companies offer interesting buy-out opportunities but, unlike in the United States, this type of transaction has, until recently, been absent from the United Kingdom. Buy-outs of quoted companies which subsequently cease to be listed (hence the term 'going private') may be undertaken to get rid of the financial and legal burdens imposed on companies by The Stock Exchange listing requirements and the cost of servicing a large number of generally remote shareholders. Additionally, such a buy-out may provide an important means by which a failing quoted company can be turned round with more highly motivated and rewarded management whilst maintaining its independence. A key role in this will be played by the new lead investors. However, as will be seen below, such buy-outs raise more contentious issues relating to, amongst other things, the conflict between management and shareholders' interests.

Financing size and legal restrictions have historically provided barriers to this type of transaction. Quoted companies, by their nature, are generally larger than their unquoted counterparts. The entry into the market-place of such US banks as Bankers Trust, Citibank and Chase has brought with it more funds and a favourable attitude to lending large sums for this type of transaction derived from North American experience.

Referring back to Figure 2.1, two broad types of buy-outs from quoted companies may be distinguished: a buy-out can occur as a defence against a hostile take-over bid or the deal is initiated without there being a competing bidder. In addition, full management buy-ins of quoted companies have also made their appearance in the United Kingdom, as seen in Chapter 1. These may take the form of the building up of an equity stake with an eventual agreed take-over offer, or may be a hostile bid, sometimes in competition with a buy-out attempt by incumbent management.

Resistance to an unwelcome bid by executive directors is not an uncommon feature of the acquisition scene in the United Kingdom. Indeed, research evidence has demonstrated the ability of a disenchanted management to prevent new owners from obtaining the returns from acquisition that were initially envisaged. Until recently, management faced with an unwelcome bid could either try to prevent the acquisition taking place, by claiming they would not co-operate with a new owner or by dissuading equity-holders from accepting the offer, or by encouraging a rival bid.

Developments in the market-place in 1985, such as the greater availability of finance, enabled the buy-out to become a feasible take-over defence. In the battle for the Debenhams Store Group in the United Kingdom, the management team mounted such a strategy, with substantial financial institution backing, rather than let the company be sold for the sums discussed. The buy-out price suggested was almost 50 per cent larger than the offer that was on the table at the time. In the event the buy-out did not succeed, but it meant the eventual acquirer having to pay a sum substantially above that initially envisaged. In June 1985 the management of Haden, a quoted engineering company did succeed in a buy-out in response to a hostile bid from Trafalgar House. The price was £56m., some £19m. above the original offer by Trafalgar House.

The £164m. buy-out attempt by the management of McCorquodale in the face of a hostile bid from Norton Opax in 1986 was, however, not successful partly because the defence was launched at a very late stage. Subsequently other defensive bids have been mounted but have not been progressed. For example, in August 1989 the management of Ward White, faced with a hostile bid from Boots, abandoned their plans to attempt a buy-out. A major problem was the reluctance by the providers of debt to fund such a transaction at a time when high interest rates were beginning to affect the retail sector and when other large buy-outs in this area were experiencing difficulties, as noted in Chapter 1.

The success of the Haden buy-out attempt, however, alerted other quoted companies to the possibilities of going private by management themselves taking the initiative and making a bid for the company. Around the same time as Haden, the management of Molins made an unsuccessful attempt to take the company private. One of the major published reasons for this proposed buy-out was the strategic opportunity offered by removal from quoted-company status. This opportunity had two aspects. First, it meant a reduction in disclosure requirements, which was seen as helpful in view of the fact that the company's major European competitors were privately owned. Second, it meant an increased ability to focus on the longer term in a sector where it takes up to seven years to develop new types of machinery. Hence, performance may be improved through the replacement of the myopic and inexpert influence of dispersed minority shareholders by a longer-term expert view that a small group of institutions together with management would be able to take. The Molins bid failed as key institutional shareholders such as M & G were reluctant to cede ownership to management, suspecting that management would make an unfair capital gain in a relatively short period of time when a stock-market re-listing was achieved. Since then there have been several successful 'going privates' each year (Table 2.7). Many of these have been helped by high levels of equity stakes held by remaining family groups or key senior executives (e.g. Virgin, Dwek, Gomme), which have reduced the problems which may arise when a firm's management, disenchanted with the City's

Table 2.7 Buy-outs of stock-market companies*

Year	Buy-out	Value(£m.)
1985	Haden	60.0
1986	Gomme	12.0
	Berkertex Holdings	21.6
1987	International Leisure	155.0
	Lee International	198.0
	Microlease	5.1
	Wickes	120.0
1988	Glass Glover	60.2
	Dwek Group	39.1
	Virgin Group	248.0
	Invergordon Distilleries	116.3
	Ariel Ind.	1.0[†]
	East Worcs Water/Biwater	4.7
1989	British Syphon	49.9
	Ryan International	69.6
	Tyzack	52.0
	Magnet	630.7
	Charles Church Developments	103.7
	Prestwich Holdings	91.0
	Illingworth Morris	74.0
	Highland Participants	72.6
	Newarthill	100.0

* Excludes buy-ins.
† Management and employee trusts already held 90 per cent after earlier offer.

Source: CMBOR.

rating of its shares, wishes to go private. Less problematical, too, are cases where significant corporate holders wish to liquidate their stakes (e.g. Wickes and Invergordon) or where the company has significantly reduced in size (e.g. Berkertex). Buy-ins of public companies also appear more acceptable as incoming management do not have insider advantages.

Several other buy-outs have involved cases where management have acted very optimistically and in these the greatest levels of concern have arisen (e.g. Magnet, British Syphon, Ryan Int. and Tyzack). Management, by refinancing the company with debt can lever up the value of the firm at the expense of existing shareholders. In addition to the potential problems with increased leverage noted in Chapter 1, certain other difficulties arise. Managers may be faced with a conflict of interest in respect of their fiduciary duties and loyalty towards shareholders. Quite apart from the distraction from running the business that the buy-out process may involve, the ability of managers to choose the timing of the bid and the price to be paid may be seen by others to amount to insider trading to the disadvantage of other shareholders. Additionally, institutional investors may oppose this kind of buy-out on the grounds that, while they may obtain a significant premium at the time of the deal, they will be asked to repurchase the shares at a higher price when the company returns to the stock market. (This issue is returned to in Chapter 7.)

It is clear that as the numbers of this type of buy-out grow, more attention will be paid to the moral and legal position of the bidding managers and pressure for safeguards to protect shareholders will increase. Some institutions, e.g. Sun Alliance, have expressed grave concern about 'going privates' although they have no objections to divestment buy-outs. Proposals made in June 1989 by the Investment Committee of the National Association of Pension Funds (NAPF), many of which have been incorporated by the Takeover Panel in late 1989, try to get round these areas of concern. Prior to a formal buy-out attempt, managers should seek shareholder permission especially where a company's resources might be used to pay fees. During the buy-out process, manage-ment should make available to shareholders the information in their proposal. If there are insurmountable difficulties in the release of confidential and competitively useful information to share-holders, NAPF argue that a buy-out should not be allowed to proceed. NAPF also suggest that detailed forecasts of profits and return on capital for at least three years should be provided to shareholders to enable them to assess the value of a management bid, and that the ultimate price of a buy-out should be related to the performance of the company in relation to these forecasts. As the position of existing non-executive directors may become difficult during a buy-out, a position of 'adviser to shareholders' ought to be created. The adviser would report on the fairness of the offer terms.

This level of concern, however, obscures the great practical difficulties which this type of buy-out involves − the need to mount the bid at a price which can expect to be recommended by non-executive directors and be favourably seen by City analysts but not encourage a competing offer; the financing requirements particularly at times of high interest rates and stock-market indices; the danger of not reaching levels of acceptance which will allow minority shareholdings to be compulsorily acquired; banking security considerations when such levels of acceptance are not achieved; the very high fees involved; and the personal risks taken by management who, if the bid fails, may be heavily out of pocket and out of a job.

Critical to the success of a 'going-private' attempt will be the initial price offered by management especially in relation to general premia applied in corporate take-overs. Research in the United States has found that the premia on 'going-private' bids are not significantly different from those in other take-overs. Despite this, institutional concern has been seen which is likely to demand new approaches. One interesting possibility is the use of some form of payment in kind. This represents a means by which the gap can be bridged between the maximum price management can pay based on their ability to raise and service sufficient external funds and what shareholders regard as a fair price. Payment in kind may take the form of convertible debt or equity ('stub equity') in the acquiring company held by the outgoing shareholders. These instruments are not serviced by cash but rather their holders receive more equity, more debt or a combination of both, depending upon performance.

Existing shareholders may be offered the choice of taking all cash, or a combination of cash and convertible instruments. Where the cash element offers a significant premium on the pre-bid share price and is close to what could be considered a fair and full cash offer, existing shareholders can share in potential growth with little risk. The combination of cash and convertible shares appears to have been a key factor in the buy-out of the publicly quoted Magnet Group in 1989 despite some considerable initial institutional opposition.

The Public Sector

As seen in Chapter 1, there has been a significant amount of both buy-out and buy-in activity from the public sector. So far this activity reached a numerical peak in 1987 with the break-up of National Bus, but has averaged almost 5 per cent of all buy-outs throughout the 1980s. There have been noticeably fewer buy-ins, partly because of the relative newness of the phenomenon, but also because of the difficulties of effecting this kind of transaction in the public sector (Table 2.8).

Public-sector buy-outs may arise from the sale of state-owned enterprises, of local authority and ancillary health services, and a whole variety of other activities including research stations, university publishing departments, development corporations, etc. The majority of such buy-outs have so far come from the privatisation of state enterprises, though over the next five years several hundred may be expected from the contracting-out of local authority and ancillary health services.

Sales of state-owned enterprises by buy-out may involve either a firm as a whole (e.g. National Freight Consortium), the complete break-up of a firm into many buy-outs (e.g. National Bus and British Technology Group), or divestment of parts while the core of the parent remains, or the divestment of service provision to employees who establish a separate entity. Several multiple sales by buy-out have been seen from British Shipbuilders, British Steel, British Rail and BL/Austin Rover as part of the process of restructuring prior to their own privatisation. For state-owned

Table 2.8 UK public-sector buy-outs and buy-ins by year

Year	Public sector Number		All UK Number		Public share %	
	Buy-outs	Buy-ins	Buy-outs	Buy-ins	Buy-outs	Buy-ins
Pre-1982	6	2	199	9	3.0	22.2
1982	8	0	238	8	3.4	0
1983	8	1	233	8	3.4	12.5
1984	4	0	238	5	1.7	0
1985	8	0	261	29	3.1	0
1986	14	0	313	48	4.5	0
1987	33	8	345	82	9.6	9.8
1988	17	1	356	94	4.8	1.1
1989 (first half)	8	0	182	63	4.4	0

Source: CMBOR.

firms in the United Kingdom, the possibilities for further buy-outs are now quite limited as much reorganisation has been completed. At the time of writing, the sell-off of the Scottish Bus Group as a series of individual transactions was just beginning. However, further possibilities exist elsewhere in the public sector, especially with respect to local authorities and ancillary health services. The Local Government Act 1988, in attempting to divorce management and political control of certain activities, introduced the possibility for buy-outs. Concern over the efficiency and effectiveness of public-sector activities has been the subject of considerable debate over a lengthy period. Complexity of many public-sector organisations may make it difficult for monitors to gain adequate information to enable them to exert control. Hence there may be a problem of control between higher and lower levels in a public-sector hierarchy. However, there may also be a divorce between senior management and the public as owners. Civil servants and ministers may pursue their own interests and/or be 'captured' by the activities they are supposed to be monitoring. The ability to change remuneration structures of public-sector employees to make them more appropriate to individual circumstances so as to provide an incentive not to engage in opportunistic behaviour may be limited by financial restrictions in certain industries and sector-wide wage structures.

In addition, public-sector ownership may involve the suppression of the spur to efficiency that might otherwise come from product and capital-market competition. Entry into a market may either be prohibited or becomes extremely difficult with the risk of prediction. Capital-market competition through the take-over mechanism is absent and the threat of bankruptcy as a check on extreme departures from cost minimisation is generally missing. Enterprise debt is typically underwritten by the state eliminating not only bankruptcy but the spur to efficiency which may come from managers being 'bonded' to meet interest obligations with little corresponding freedom to indulge their own non-profit interests. All the foregoing is reinforced by the problems in monitoring and reward structures which arise from ambiguity in the objective functions of public-sector firms.

Buy-outs may provide a means of resolving issues involved in the control of state enterprises while at the same time helping to avoid some of the difficulties with other privatisation approaches. Buy-outs may have a greater positive impact upon internal efficiency because of the increased incentive which derives from a greater level of managerial and employee ownership than is likely from a stock-market flotation. Moreover, buy-outs invariably involve higher levels of debt financing than companies subject to stock-market flotation. To the extent that debt financing carries with it a commitment to meet predetermined repayment schedules, managers may have greater pressure to perform. The alternative may be failure and loss of employment. However, it is important to be clear at the outset that buy-outs may not be suitable or feasible in all circumstances.

Sale of a whole state enterprise as one buy-out may be appropriate where it does not meet the market conditions for stock market flotation. Break-up on privatisation may be appropriate in geographically spread 'people' businesses where co-ordination is most important at the local level and where activities provided centrally could be replaced by some form of market transaction or by local provision, as, for example, in the bus industry. Within state-holding companies it seems likely that there will be a set of activities which are not of central concern but which are bound by financial constraints on the whole enterprise and where management are also constrained in their ability to take action appropriate to local circumstances. Similarly, divestments of peripheral activities which do not trade with the main parts of a state enterprise may yield benefits to the entity concerned and to the vendor through the removal of control costs and the reduction of organisational complexity.

Of particular interest are those areas which will continue to trade with or provide a service to the divesting unit, either as inputs to state-sector firms or as services such as refuse collection, leisure-centre management etc., in the local-authority sector. Hence the issues involved relate to how to gain most from reductions in internal control problems, whilst at the same time maintaining a contractual relationship which provides for an adequate quality of service at a price which does not leave the vendor the victim of opportunistic behaviour by management in the divested entity. It is here that buy-outs raise particularly interesting possibilities. Of key importance is the nature of the trading relationship. The existence of non-routine tasks, with a degree of specialist knowledge required, few competitors and an asymmetry of dependence between vendor and the entity sold, are crucial factors. Where these criteria are met there may be important transactional advantages through close co-ordination across separate entities. A priori, buy-outs may provide a more appropriate basis for such co-ordination than sale to an already established independent firm. An existing firm with a relatively wide customer base may be less dependent on a particular contract with a state firm or local authority than are former employees. Additionally, a buy-out may at the outset provide a means of avoiding quality-control and compliance-monitoring problems than contracting with an existing firm since it may be easier to establish compatible perceptions of what is required for an acceptable standard of service to be achieved and to establish close working relationships. Separation of activities may convey a credible message that the trading partner is no longer responsible as lender of last resort. Hence the possibility that poor performance will not be bailed out (or may provoke a take-over bid) is made much clearer. In local authorities, where in-house teams win tenders against outside bidders but remain as employees, the possibility for poor performance to be rescued exists.

Detailed contractual specifications may still be required if value for money is to be obtained, including the possibility of reopening the tendering process. A potential problem exists at the time of the buy-out since incumbents with specialist knowledge may be able to negotiate highly favourable terms. Normal due diligence pro-cedures at the time of sale may resolve some of these problems, together with fair competitive tendering for the service or entity. Also, care may be needed in ensuring competitive tendering does occur, since outside bidders may be reluctant to bid for contracts where they perceive a serious proposition by an in-house team, since the in-house team, as employees, has an informational advantage in contractual requirements. While this is a problem that local authorities need to resolve, successful buy-outs also need to consider carefully how they may develop the business in order to reduce the vulnerability which may come from being dependent upon a single contract.

The manner in which the buy-out is constructed may also contribute to a minimisation of potential control problems. One possibility is to seek tenders to sell the assets of the company separately from the contracts to provide a service (e.g. the sale by British Rail of Doncaster wagon works) and to stipulate that the contracts require close co-operation with the vendor. In this kind of situation the vendor may be highly knowledgeable about the products required.

Alternatively, and particularly in the case of state enterprises, the vendor parent may take a part in financing the buy-out through deferred payments (based on future performance), loans or retentions of equity stakes. Such interests serve several functions. First, they may enable separation to occur where otherwise insufficient funds could be raised. Second, where an equity stake is involved the vendor may limit the problem of selling at too low a price where incumbent management are in possession of greater information and obtain a share in future gains. Third, it may enable the vendor to maintain a stronger lever on the performance of the former subsidiary. In the United Kingdom, important equity stakes have been maintained by BL/Austin Rover and British Steel in the buy-outs they have effected where important trading continues, but not with those peripheral entities which have been sold.

A wider spread of employee share ownership, possibly effected through an Employee Share Ownership Trust, may help improve motivation and performance. It may also help to reduce trade-union resistance to privatisation. The wider share ownership possibilities of buy-outs may be especially important where individual efforts and widespread entrepreneurial skills are key to a firm's performance. However, the ability of the firm and management to survive as an independent entity need to be taken into account in considering a buy-out. In addition, the need to reassure the public that sale is taking place at a fair price may mean that a buy-out fails in competition with an outside bidder.

Conclusions

Buy-outs are seen to come from a variety of sources. As legal and financial barriers are removed, types of buy-out which were not possible in the first wave of the phenomenon now become feasible. Add to these sources the demographic features described in Chapter 1 and the variety of ways of structuring the deal, as will be seen in Chapter 5, and it will be clear that there is a distinct lack of homogeneity in the type of company that is suitable for buying out. However, certain definite ground rules present themselves when assessing the feasibility of a buy-out, which are addressed in Chapter 3.

CHAPTER 3

Preparation for buy-out

In order to obtain funding from a prospective financier, the buy-out team and their advisers need to prepare a convincing business plan. This plan provides an analysis of the history of the business, its current position within the market, and management's best estimates of its prospects for the future. The first part of this chapter reviews the principal issues which need to be covered in the business plan. The second part uses an annotated example of an actual company to show the nature of the financial statements which will be required.

The Issues to be Covered

A prospective funder needs to know the buy-out's current financial position, how it got there, and where it expects to go in the future. Unlike very young companies, almost all prospective buy-outs have some kind of trading track record to enable a financing institution to make a reasonably objective decision about whether a potentially sound commercial activity exists. Of course, in those buy-outs from actual or near receivership the financial track record may appear quite damning. But here, past information may help highlight what has gone wrong and what may be required to rectify the position.

The past provides the context for an assessment of the current financial position of the firm. Such an analysis enables a judgement to be made as to whether present performance is noticeably out of line with recent trends. However, before forecasts of the future financial position can be made, certain other questions require answers. Specifically, the matters to be examined concern the following:

1. The nature of existing trading resources (customers, products, suppliers, order levels, etc.).
2. The nature of existing human resources (management and employees).
3. The nature of existing physical capital resources (buildings, equipment, etc.).
4. The nature of existing organisational resources (management, production and control systems).
5. The nature of existing financial resources (including financial control systems).

The importance of each of these factors is as follows.

Existing Trading Resources
Unlike completely new firms, buy-outs have been servicing a market with established products for some time before the transfer of ownership. However, companies which become buy-outs may have been sold either because they have underperformed or because, though profitable, they no longer fit the parent's strategic direction. In the first instance there is a need to assess what can be changed to improve the post-buy-out trading position. A distinction may need to be made between performance problems relating to trading resources and those which concern managerial weaknesses, to which we return below. For those companies which are profitable but do not fit the parent's strategy, consideration needs to be given to the future prospects for existing products and for entry into new markets with new or current products.

The general market conditions will be affected by macro-economic factors at home, and abroad if exports are envisaged, as well as factors which relate specifically to the industry. The growth, both actual and potential, of the market needs to be assessed, as well as the firm's position in that market. This requires consideration of the extent and nature of competition within the firm's particular niche, including the relative stength and market-share position of the firm in relation to its competitors. The relative stability of the market is also important given the likely need for the bought-out company to meet regular finance servicing costs. The likelihood of technological change involving new products or production processes, together with possible import penetration will affect market stability. Where the potential buy-out candidate itself wishes to introduce new products and enter new markets after the transfer of ownership, careful assessment is required, the more so when the new developments are further away from the traditional markets and expertise. If these new products are planned to be produced soon after buy-out, evidence of thorough research of the market-potential entry-pricing strategy and entry costs will be required. Given the serious adverse impact upon a buy-out's ability to service its external funding should a major new product venture fail, potential institutional investors will give such proposals serious scrutiny particularly for those products outside existing areas of expertise. However, they may also be very positive in perceiving the need for new product development and make suggestions for the directions it may take together with an allowance in the financial structure for the investment costs required. The development of new products and entry into new markets are very difficult tasks and the buy-out team need to avoid over-enthusiasm in their newly gained independence to embark on plans which are not sound.

While, by their nature, buy-outs will have existing products with established prices, changes in the cost base following the transfer of ownership may provide the possibility for a more competitive pricing strategy or at least a reassessment of the basis for current prices. Pricing strategies for proposed new products also require careful attention, since these will affect market share, profitability and the rate of growth of sales. The relevant costs for each new product need to be calculated and sensitivity analysis conducted in order to estimate the effect of different price mark-ups on market penetration, and different market-growth assumptions on profitability. A balance may also need to be struck between the quality and refinement of a product (and hence its cost) and what the market demands at a price which provides the firm with an acceptable return. There may be important scope for differentiation of product characteristics and prices in order to serve different, market segments.

Existing Human Resources
Human resources embrace both the management team and the general body of employees. The management team is crucial to guiding the buy-out to meet its financing commitments and its longer-term development. An assessment needs to be made of the ability and commitment of all team members, their experience and the overall breadth of skills of the team as a whole. Such an evaluation may be difficult, requiring as it does judgement as to

whether managers who are currently employees of a larger group, or who have not previously experienced the complete running of an independent firm, are going to cope after the transfer of ownership. Clearly, careful scrutiny of their track records, particularly those of prospective chief executives, is an important element in the process. Convincing explanations as to why an under-achieving subsidiary's performance will be significantly transformed by the same management team when it becomes independent will need to be produced. A not uncommon argument is that managers have been restricted by the procedures and costs of central group services and pursuing initiatives and adapting to market changes in a timely fashion.

The typical buy-out team generally has a clearly identified leader who combines both entrepreneurial and managerial skills and who may be crucial in guiding the buy-out through its transitional phase. In addition, representatives of each of the key functions of the firm may be expected to form part of the buy-out team. Depending upon the size of the buy-out and the nature of the markets served, there will be variations in the number of senior managers who form part of the co-ordinating team and who are equity-holders. Hence, for example, a buy-out with a number of geographically spread distribution outlets may wish to give the managers of each outlet an equity stake to help ensure they perform to the level necessary for the firm to meet its financial targets. Equity stakes may also be important in minimising turnover among those managers below the senior level who might otherwise see their career enhancement prospects to be restricted after buy-out. However, the larger the team, the greater co-ordination problems are likely to be. Hence, a feasible option may be for a key team to negotiate the deal and hold the most senior positions, with less senior members receiving a more modest equity stake. This level of managers may either receive equity at the time of the buy-out or at a subsequent date through the use of an Executive Share Option Scheme.

The choice of team members is a delicate issue. Some members, perhaps nearing retirement, may wish to leave at this point of their own accord. Others may express a desire, or be invited, to remain with another part of the vendor group. Those not invited by the initiators of the buy-out to be part of the team may leave the company. Such managers may have been identified as having a key subsidiary role to play and it is necessary to be sure that they can be replaced.

Gaps in the team which arise because a particular function was provided at group level may need to be filled through the recruitment of a manager from outside the firm. It will need to be decided whether this manager becomes a member of the team on the same terms as the original members or receives a performance-related remuneration package.

The buy-out provides a break at which the size of the labour force and the tasks they perform can be reassessed. Where a buy-out is from receivership, selective re-employment to provide a reduced but more appropriate workforce may be possible. However, the conditions attached to the Transfer of Undertakings Regulations will need to be observed, as explained in more detail in Chapter 7. Buy-outs of subsidiaries of larger groups may previously have been constrained in their flexible use of personnel by the need to follow group policies or to meet collective agreements made at a group level. These constraints may be questioned post-buy-out. There may be opportunities, for example, to reduce the proportion of indirect employees. The need to service relatively high levels of debt is likely to provide the extra spur to examining the appropriate levels of employees.

Beyond more junior levels of management, it may also be wished to give consideration to extending equity participation to the general body of employees, in order to increase motivation and commitment to the buy-out. Traditionally, it has often been difficult to include the general body of employees at the time the deal is negotiated because of the complexities involved and particularly when the deal has to be completed quickly against a competing external bidder. Even where there has been an offer to all employees to purchase shares with a minimum investment of, say, £200, the take-up rate is often low. Part of the equity may be set aside for distribution to employees at a later date. An internal share market will usually need to be created to enable existing employees to sell their holdings and monitor developments in the share's value, and also to enable new employees or those changing their minds to obtain an equity stake. Many companies have waited until flotation of shares on a stock market to extend an opportunity to buy shares to the wider body of employees. An alternative route may be to establish an Employee Share Ownership Trust (ESOT), which may borrow funds to purchase shares on behalf of all employees, distributing them on an individual basis as the borrowings are paid down out of contributions from future earnings. Under such a scheme employees do not necessarily have to make a share purchase at the outset, although a modest sum may be required to signify commitment. The ESOT may act as the share buffer to enable the internal share market to work. This form of scheme is considered in more detail in Chapter 7.

Existing Physical Capital Resources
The nature of existing physical capital resources concerns the amount, type and quality of machinery, equipment (including production processes) and premises. It is necessary to assess the suitability of these resources to enable the firm to continue as a viable entity and perhaps adjust the purchase price or the bundle of assets purchased where this is not satisfactorily the case. This may be particularly true where the business has been running down for many years, either because of impending receivership or because it was starved of cash by a parent. In addition, the change implied by the transfer of ownership may also provide the opportunity to alter the nature and extent of capital resources that the firm owns.

Premises provide both use for the firm's productive activity, but also security for senior debt. Premises need to be assessed in terms of their suitability for existing production, and their flexibility for expected future needs. The saleability of premises may be important in assessing their value for security against loans but it is also a measure of the feasibility available to the bought-out firm. The firm may be able to make financing adjustments through property sales if profit and cash flows fall significantly behind target. Saleable property may also enable relocation to occur more easily where this is deemed necessary. Freehold property may be easier to sell, for example, than leasehold premises should the need arise. The firm may also benefit from increases in the value of property after the buy-out has taken place. However, the issues are not so clear-cut and there may be important disadvantages in owning premises. The cost of rental can be significantly lower than the equivalent cost of the extra borrowing required to purchase property. Moreover, as the buy-out is unlikely to obtain 100 per cent financial facilities in relation to the purchase of the property it would in essence be eating into the working capital requirement raised to support the fixed assets. Additionally, in traditional industries, the buildings would have limited alternative use, hence substantially reducing resale value and their value as security. On forced sale, the problem becomes even more acute. Hence in some buy-outs it may be appropriate to find a means of not taking on premises, possibly through a sale and leaseback arrangement. Sale and leaseback may also be a means of reducing external borrowing needs in respect of other fixed assets such as transport fleets, although the Company will need to consider the tax consequences of sale. On a going-concern basis, it is unlikely that provision will have been made either for tax on potential capital gains or for the clawback of capital allowances.

Where receivership is involved, management may face a difficult time in negotiating with the receiver for what they really want, as the assets in which management are interested may not represent the important parcel of assets for the receiver, in the context of the debenture deed. In buy-outs on divestment, where the business to be bought does not have a clear independent identity, care is required in ensuring that what is purchased is viable outside the corporate umbrella.

In terms of equipment and production processes, the need is to ensure that capacity is of a sufficient technological level and physical state of repair so that products can be produced of appropriate quality and price to meet the demands of the market-place. While former subsidiaries starved of investment funds by their parents may require replacement capital expenditure, market conditions may not require this to be latest-generation technology. Reconditioned equipment may be satisfactory and available at lower prices. The bought-out company may, however, compete on the basis of factors other than production with the latest tech-nology. While there may be scope for extra funding for investment in the original financial structure of the buy-out, the ability of cash flows to service the costs involved will limit the amount which can be provided. Alternatively, the deal may need to be structured with more equity-type funds which do not demand such a high level of regular dividend payments but which may give lower equity stakes to management. The ability to make this kind of adjustment will depend upon its acceptability to management and the willingness of institutional investors to structure a deal in this way. A further option is to structure a deal with a clear view to re-financing the company in the medium term in order to meet anticipated requirements for investment in new equipment.

Existing Organisational Resources
Existing organisational resources involve the nature of the manage-ment structure and its accompanying control systems. In some buy-outs from larger groups, services previously provided centrally will need to be replaced. This may mean the introduction of personnel to carry out such functions or they may be able to be provided

through a market relationship with the buy-out's financial adviser or another part of the funding institution. Occasionally, the separate provision of services may be dispensed with, as an existing manager can carry out the tasks. Significant cost reductions may in any case be obtained.

The management structure may be incomplete because services have been provided at group level, but it may also be inappropriate to independent circumstances in a particular market environment as the previous owner imposed a uniform structure across the whole company. An assessment of the structure which will provide the necessary coverage and flexibility after buy-out is needed.

Existing Financial Resources and Control Systems

Existing financial resources include the current long-term capital structure, working capital and taxation liabilities. There is a need to ascertain that financial resources do not present a serious impediment to the viability of the business as an independent entity. If such is the case, solutions have to be found before the buy-out can proceed. The finance raised on buy-out should cover not only the purchase price of the company but also adequate working-capital facilities, and sufficient long-term capital to allow a regular capital-expenditure programme to be maintained.

Financial control systems are important in respect of the need to monitor closely actual performance against budget, for keeping tight control over debtors and creditors, for the negotiation of day-to-day borrowing requirements and for investment appraisal. Control over debtors and creditors has important implications for cash flow in the business, which in turn is crucial for meeting debt-servicing commitments.

Pressure from creditors for early payment may arise where suppliers experience uncertainty about the newly independent entity. Debtors too may exert pressure through the extension of payment periods. In both cases buy-outs may suffer where they are relatively small compared to the customer or supplier but where each accounts for a significant proportion of the buy-out's supplies and sales. Detailed scrutiny of the debtor and creditor profiles may be expected both to ascertain the degree of dependence on particular companies and to identify existing and potential problem areas. It is not unusual to find customers and suppliers who are supportive of the management's attempts to go it alone. For example, in one case of a divestment, major suppliers put pressure on the parent to sell to management rather than an unknown external purchaser. Similarly, suppliers may help in the provision of consignment stock. Where advance warning is available to the management it has often proved a useful device to nurture the support of customers and suppliers before the change in ownership, particularly in the case of buy-outs from receivership. The CMBOR survey confirmed that the move to independence frequently improves customer and supplier relationships, with less than 2 per cent of the sample actually recording worse relationships. Significantly customer relationships were, however, more likely to improve in divestment than retirement cases. Receivership cases were, as might be expected, more vulnerable to the loss of customers and suppliers.

The above analysis is important, partly in assessing the commercial viability of the business, partly in seeing if any lessons can be learned and applied to the future, and partly to temper the over-optimism that often exists in assessments of future prospects. However, though the track record of the company provides an explanation of how it arrived at today's position, of itself it may not provide a reliable guide to the future. Given the changes that will occur after the buy-out, the loss of parental protection, changes in the capital structure, and substantial reorganisation, it is necessary to provide best estimates of future performance. The current position plus an appraisal of likely trends in demand for the company's products, sources and strength of competition and other economic factors provide the basis for three main statements:

- a profit forecast for one year forward in detail, with at least outline forecasts for up to two further years;
- a balance-sheet forecast for one year ahead in detail, with at least outline forecasts for up to two further years;
- a cash-flow forecast for one year ahead in detail and an outline forecast for a further year.

These forecasts will build on past trends and will need to take account of seasonalities in sales and costs, the impact of development plans already in progress and the likely effects of extraordinary items. However, the most important element is the assumption on which the forecasts are based.

It is quite possible to make even the most hopeless of cases look like a viable proposition, but convincing a financial adviser or institution that near miraculous improvements in performance can in fact be achieved may be rather more difficult. The following specific kinds of assumptions need to be clearly stated:

- percentage growth in each product market served by the firm, by volume and value;
- extent of and changes in market share for each product;

- the margin on each product;
- expected inflation rates;
- expected interest rates;
- expected capital expenditure;
- expected working-capital levels;
- expected stock levels, potential supply problems and the effects on raw-material costs;
- expected creditor cycles;
- expected debtor cycles;
- expected impact of ending of capital repayment holidays on post-buy-out financial position;
- expected extraordinary items, including the impact of reorganisation costs on financial statements;
- effect of exchange-rate fluctuations where significant overseas trade exists;
- taxation implications;
- the expected net benefits from the removal of any head-office management service changes.

This might seem a formidable list, but a capable management ought to have a definite view about each aspect, and indeed they are likely to be subject to probing on these areas by financial advisers and institutions.

Additionally, given the uncertainty about the future it is vital to provide estimates of the effects of changes in the assumptions on the financial statements. For example, pressure on creditor payment and extended debtor cycles may have substantial effects on funding requirements, and the range of possibilities needs to be delineated. Such sensitivity analysis provides an important guide to the underlying stability of the business. Even where conservative assumptions about the future are made, uncertainty will remain and unfavourable effects on profits and cash flow may result. Tables 3.1 and 3.2 show the experiences of 182 management buy-outs surveyed by CMBOR in these respects. The buy-outs were completed between mid-1983 and the first quarter of 1986. Comparative figures from a survey of 111 buy-outs completed before mid-1983 are also included in the tables. On balance the effects on profits have tended to be favourable, with market and product developments, productivity and profit-margin increases and overhead reductions being most notable. However, for some buy-outs market factors coupled with depressed margins have had adverse effects on profits. Firms may particularly notice these effects where they were anticipating significant improvements on

Table 3.1 Post-buy-out effects on profits

Factor	Favourable		Unfavourable	
	Before mid-1983[1] %	Mid-1983–86[2] %	Before mid-1983[1] %	Mid-1983–86[2] %
Market	20.7	23.0	13.5	12.6
Productivity	17.1	9.3	–	0.5
Overheads	16.2	13.7	–	2.2
Margins	7.2	11.5	10.8	3.3
Purchasing policies	7.2	2.2	1.8	–
Product development	4.5	9.8	1.8	0.5
Extraordinary items	4.5	2.2	9.9	4.4
Financing	2.7	3.8	1.8	3.3
Currency variations	1.8	1.6	1.8	3.3

Base for percentages = 111 (before mid-1983), 182 (mid-1983–86)

Sources:
1. M. Wright and J. Coyne, *Management Buy-outs*, Croom-Helm, Beckenham, 1985 (this survey was the first comprehensive survey of UK buy-outs).
2. CMBOR survey of buy-outs between mid-1983 and the first quarter of 1986

Table 3.2 Cash flow problems post buy-out

	Sample	
	Before mid-1983[1]	Mid-1983–86[2]
Percentage of companies encountering cash-flow problems	31.6	33.3
Factor:	% of Companies	% of companies
Not achieving expected profit margins	17.1	18.0
Stock levels	7.2	10.9
Interest payments on bank overdraft	8.1	8.7
Interest payments on long-term loans	8.1	8.2
Bad debts, etc.	12.6	6.0
Dividends to institutions	n.a.	2.2
Other	10.1	10.9

Sources:
1. M. Wright and J. Coyne, *Management Buy-outs*, Croom-Helm, Beckenham, 1985.
2. CMBOR survey of buy-outs between mid-1983 and the first quarter of 1986.

the previous track record to meet a heavy financing burden but where the recession has been more prolonged than expected. It is particularly noteworthy that between the two surveys recovery of profit margins, product development and improved market conditions have increased in importance, while productivity growth and overhead reductions have fallen. In respect of post-buy-out cash flow, inability to achieve expected margins has had the most severe adverse effect. Problems in maintaining adequate control over stock levels is seen as the second most important factor, and taken together with the problem of bad debts, emphasises the need to develop robust control systems in advance of the buy-out. For some buy-outs, interest payments on finance appear to have had a more severe impact than anticipated, though encouragingly over two-thirds of buy-outs had no post-buy-out cash-flow problems. Some 37.1 per cent of companies in the sample reported a need to raise further finance for one or more reasons after buy-out, highlighting the need to think carefully about adequate funding at the time the deal is completed. The reasons for requiring further finance were greater sales volume (19.1 per cent) higher capital expenditure (12 per cent), to make an acquisition (10.4 per cent) and failure to meet original targets (4.9 per cent). We return to post-buy-out issues in Chapter 8.

Management buy-ins

While the above analysis is also relevant to management buy-ins, these do pose a number of difficulties. In particular, as new management are coming in from outside the firm, by definition, they are less likely than a buy-out team to be as fully aware of the true state of existing resources and potential problems. This difficulty may particularly arise where a buy-in attempt is hostile since the would-be acquirers may not be able to obtain access to reliable and detailed information and the process of due diligence may be more difficult to achieve. The issue may be especially acute in the case of public buy-ins. The problem may be lessened where the buy-in is an agreed bid for a family business where the proprietors wish to see the firm continue as an independent entity.

Where incumbent management are attempting a buy-out in competition with a buy-in bid, further problems arise, particularly if the firm is not underperforming. However, if existing management have not been extracting the full potential of the business, investors may prefer a buy-in, as has been seen in some prominent recent public deals such as Isosceles/Gateway and Lowndes Queensway.

The buy-in opportunity may arise in a firm requiring turnround and if this is the case the price to be paid should reflect the work to be done and the risks associated with such a deal; the assets of the business may not be in as good a condition as anticipated and the cash flow may prove to be less strong, either because of the costs of turnround or because market conditions make turnround more difficult to achieve than expected.

Internal management may be removed, at least in part, in a buy-in target that has been underperforming. However, good elements of existing management may be retained to complete the buy-in team especially in areas where the buy-in team may lack expertise. The buy-in team itself will typically possess stronger entre-preneurial skills than the average buy-out team, but may contain certain weaknesses. The team may not have worked together before, may have varying levels of commitment (especially those managers planning to leave existing careers), and may not be complete. Financial institutions will need to assess these strengths and possibly wish to take a greater monitoring role after the transaction than is true for a buy-out.

Perhaps the major difficulty is in finding a target to which the incoming management is suitable and at an acceptable price (taking account of the higher levels of risk) where the vendor is willing to sell to an unknown set of individuals who may or may not have worked in the sector before. The role of the financing institution is clearly of critical importance in giving the team this financial respectability.

Midlands Plating and Finishing Ltd (MPF): An Annotated Example

What follows illustrates and comments on the financial part of the buy-out proposal for an actual company, the real name being disguised to protect confidentiality.

MPF is a growing company engaged in the business of metal plating, grinding, polishing and applying various coatings to customers' own materials. The five senior managers of the company propose to purchase it from its parent company, Lightfoot plc. Lightfoot plc has indicated that it is willing to receive such a proposal, as MPF is now considered peripheral to the parent's main activities, following a strategic review. Initial discussions have taken place concerning the purchase price and an offer of £4.3m. is to be made. In addition the cost of the buy-out is estimated at £200,000. The management team of MPF is seeking financial support for the buy-out and it is proposed to fund it as follows:

			£(000)
Ordinary shares	−	Management	120
	−	Institutions	100
			220
Redeemable preference shares			930
			1,150
Loan			1,000
Cash surplus			1,212
Overdraft			1,138
			£4,500

This funding structure would be provided in order to illustrate the ability of the company to service it. In practice management teams should be wary of presenting a fixed structure since bankers and investors will wish to formulate their own.

Repayment of the £1m. loan (secured on debtors) would be made within three years, at which point MPF would seek a flotation or other means of raising funds which would put a value on the business. At that point, with MPF approaching full maturity, the intention would be to diversify into other related businesses. In order to justify its case to the financing institution, MPF's management have prepared the following information:

- an adjusted company balance sheet to show the effects of changes in financing (Table 3.3);
- turnover and profits for the past three years and forecasts for the next three (Table 3.4);
- detailed monthly profit forecast for the first year after buy-out (Table 3.5);
- detailed monthly cash-flow forecast for the first year after buy-out (Table 3.6);
- detailed summary of profit forecasts for the three years after buy-out (Table 3.7);
- detailed summary of cash-flow forecasts for the three years after buy-out (Table 3.8);
- balance sheets for the current year and the first three years after buy-out (Table 3.9);
- summary of expected fixed-asset movements after buy-out (Table 3.10);
- detailed assumptions to forecasts (Table 3.11).

The effects of the proposed purchase and its accompanying funding arrangements require a redrafting of the existing balance sheet. The major changes in Table 3.3 are in respect of the financing arrangements noted earlier, but certain other changes are worth noting. First, the time of the buy-out provides the opportunity to introduce improvements to buildings, amounting to some £336,000. Second, these improvements increase the amount of the inter-company loan from the parent to £3,555,000, which is repaid as part of the £4,300,000 purchase price. With net assets of £56,000, the balance of the purchase price and the costs together give rise to a figure for goodwill on acquisition of £889,000.

The summary of actual turnover and trading profit for the past two years, the current year and the forecast for the next three years, is shown in Table 3.4. Turnover and trading profit are presented as increasing steadily over the period, with turnover doubling and trading profit tripling in the period 19X8 to 19X3. The

Table 3.3 Midlands Plating and Finishing Ltd: adjustments to opening balance sheet

	Closing 31.12.19X0 (£000)	Adjustments (£000)		Day one 1.1.19X0 (£000)
Fixed assets	1,956	336	Buildings	2,292
Goodwill	–	889	see note below	889
Stocks	61			61
Debtors	1,965			1,965
Cash	1,212	(1,212)	see text	–
	3,238			2,026
Creditors	(1,197)			(1,197)
Overdraft	–	1,138	see text	(1,138)
Corporation Tax	(260)			(260)
	(1,457)			(2,595)
Net current assets/(liabilities)	1,781			(569)
Inter-company	(3,219)	(336) / 3,555	Buildings see Table 3.10	
Deferrred tax	(462)			(462)
	56			2,150
Share capital: Ordinary	10			220
Preference	–			930
	10			1,150
Reserves	46			–
Loan	–			1,000
	56			2,150

Note:
Purchase price	(£000)
Net assets	56
Inter-company loan repaid	3,555
Goodwill	889
	4,500

Table 3.4 Midlands Plating and Finishing Ltd: past results and forecasts (£000)

	Audited 19X8	Audited 19X9	Draft 19X0	Forecast 19X1	Forecast 19X2	Forecast 19X3
Turnover	6,572	7,520	9,805	11,117	12,638	13,937
Trading profit	467	439	652	797	1,112	1,238
Lightfoot plc management charge	(95)	(114)	–	–	–	–
Bank interest	(105)*	(115)*	(125)*	(161)	(118)	(172)
Loan interest	–	–	–	(144)	(144)	–
HP interest	–	–	–	(27)	(91)	(149)
Profit before tax	267	210	527	465	759	917

* Notional rate of interest on net debt.

basis for these expected results is considered below. Of particular importance in the Table are the effects of removing significant parental management charges and the switch from notional rates of interest on previous funding to the new arrangements. Under the figures presented, MPF, after a dip in post-interest pre-tax profits in the year of transition, is shown to be comfortably generating the funds to service its new financial structure.

The detail behind the forecast profit for the first year after the buy-out is shown in Table 3.5, while Table 3.6 shows the cash-flow implications. In the first month a significant net loss is expected followed generally for the remainder of the year by fluctuating profit levels. Notice that these fluctuations appear to relate to distinct seasonal effects in sales requiring accompanying increases in labour payments. The effects of fluctuating sales are reflected in the cash-flow forecast of Table 3.6. The net profits from Table 3.5 are adjusted for depreciation to derive estimates of monthly cash generated from trading.

To obtain the full cash position, changes in debtors and creditors, taxation, HP balances and asset purchases need to be taken into account. Debtor and creditor figures are generally seen to move in different directions and at different rates, and reflect differences between collection periods for the former and payment periods for the latter. It is here that the need for good financial control systems is crucial to the maintenance of a stable cash flow, keeping the overdraft within borrowing limits. It is also important to include the effect of corporation and value-added tax payments and of dividends. Where a management buy-out occurs via the asset-purchase route (see Chapter 7) the effect on cash flow of VAT on the purchase price needs to be taken into account (a VAT concession may be available in certain cases).

Table 3.5 Midlands Plating and Finishing Ltd: profit forecast for the year ending 31 December 19X1

(£000)

	Jan	Feb	Mar	Apr	May	Jun	July	Aug	Sep	Oct	Nov	Dec	Total
Sales	781	804	812	1,054	799	863	1,004	801	944	1,271	1,112	872	11,117
Works overheads	235	207	205	265	206	219	268	209	223	277	230	214	2,758
Labour	291	274	264	347	270	293	359	269	313	408	347	313	3,748
Sub-contract	36	37	41	60	44	46	55	43	54	84	72	55	627
Gross profit	219	286	302	382	279	305	322	280	354	502	463	290	3,984
Selling, distribution and admin. overheads	283	242	238	290	234	243	299	239	245	336	278	259	3,186
HP interest	–	–	–	–	1	1	1	1	5	6	6	6	27
Loan interest	12	12	12	12	12	12	12	12	12	12	12	12	144
Bank charges	14	13	14	15	13	15	12	11	12	13	14	16	162
Total overheads	309	267	264	317	260	271	324	263	274	367	310	293	3,519
Net profit (loss), before tax	(90)	19	38	65	19	34	(2)	17	80	135	153	(3)	465
Goodwill written off													(90)
Corporation tax													(252)
Deferred tax movement													83
Preference dividends													(81)
Profit available to ordinary shareholders													125

Table 3.6 Midlands Plating and Finishing Ltd: cash-flow forecast for the year ending 31 December 19X1

	Jan	Feb	Mar	Apr	May	Jun	July	Aug	Sep	Oct	Nov	Dec	Total
							(£000)						
Profit	(90)	19	38	65	19	34	(2)	17	80	135	153	(3)	465
Depreciation	58	45	46	59	46	46	58	47	45	62	49	49	610
Cash generated from trading	(32)	64	84	124	65	80	56	64	125	197	202	46	1,075
* Net working capital movement	163	(197)	(118)	80	(194)	150	90	(178)	(27)	22	(342)	230	(321)
* Corporation tax	–	–	–	–	–	–	–	–	–	(260)	–	–	(260)
Capital expenditure	–	(15)	(15)	–	(100)	–	(20)	(62)	(525)	(113)	–	–	(850)
* Net HP borrowing/(payments)	–	11	11	(1)	73	(2)	13	43	379	73	(10)	(10)	580
Preference dividend and related ACT	–	–	–	–	–	(27)	(11)	–	–	–	–	(54)	(92)
	163	(201)	(122)	79	(221)	121	72	(197)	(173)	(278)	(352)	166	(943)
Cash generated	131	(137)	(38)	203	(156)	201	128	(133)	(48)	(81)	(150)	212	132
Opening cash	(1,138)	(1,007)	(1,144)	(1,182)	(979)	(1,135)	(934)	(806)	(939)	(987)	(1,068)	(1,218)	(1,138)
Closing cash	(1,007)	(1,144)	(1,182)	(979)	(1,135)	(934)	(806)	(939)	(987)	(1,068)	(1,218)	(1,006)	(1,006)

* Supporting documentation detailing the construction of these figures will need to be available to investors and bankers.

Beyond one year ahead it is difficult to provide reliable detailed monthly profit-and-loss accounts and cash-flow forecasts, particularly with the kind of fluctuations in activity which have been seen to take place throughout the year. However, it is necessary to provide a detailed analysis of annual profit and cash-flow forecasts for the three years ahead, to enable trends to be assessed. Table 3.7 provides the forecast profit information, and shows an expected increase in the gross margin on sales over the period. Non-manufacturing overheads are also expected to increase by less than the growth of turnover and although HP interest and bank charges are substantial, the company will benefit from the ending of loan-interest payments in year three. Retained profit also demonstrates a substantial expected improvement, though the effect of tax charges is particularly noticeable in 19X3.

In presenting the forecast cash flow, Table 3.8 starts by taking the net profit before tax of Table 3.7 and adjusting it for depreciation. The remainder of the table summarises the other movements. Note that the loan is repaid in full at the end of 19X2, giving an overdraft position of £1.5m. The final set of forecast figures concerns the balance sheets for three years ahead which, together with the adjusted position at the time of the changes in ownership, are shown in Table 3.9.

Table 3.7 Midlands Plating and Finishing Ltd: summary of profit forecasts 19X1–19X3

	19X1 (£000)	19X2 (£000)	19X3 (£000)
Sales	11,117	12,638	13,937
Works overheads	2,758	2,968	3,123
Labour	3,748	4,229	4,735
Sub-contract	627	669	757
Gross profit	3,984	4,772	5,322
Gross profit/sales	35.8%	37.8%	38.2%
Selling, distribution and administration overheads	3,186	3,540	3,964
Contingency	–	120	120
HP Interest	27	91	149
Loan interest	144	144	–
Bank charges	162	118	172
Total overheads	3,519	4,013	4,405
Net profit before tax	465	759	917
Goodwill written off	(90)	(90)	(90)
Tax charge	(169)	(296)	(355)
Preference dividend	(81)	(108)	(108)
Retained profit	125	265	364

Table 3.8 Midlands Plating and Finishing Ltd: summary of cash-flow forecasts 19X1–19X3

	19X1 (£000)	19X2 (£000)	19X3 (£000)
Profit	465	759	917
Depreciation	610	719	743
	1,075	1,478	1,660
Net working capital movement	(321)	(196)	(118)
Corporation tax	(260)	(252)	(387)
Capital expenditure	(850)	(725)	(725)
Net HP borrowing/(payments)	580	370	265
Preference dividend and related ACT	(92)	(144)	(108)
Working capital	(943)	(947)	(1,078)
Cash generated	132	531	582
Opening cash	(1,138)	(1,006)	(1,475)
Closing cash	(1,006)	(475)	(893)
Loan repayment 31.12.X2		(1,000)	
		(1,475)	

Table 3.9 Midlands Plating and Finishing Ltd: opening and forecast balance sheets 19X1–19X3

	As at 31 December			
	19X0 (£000)	19X1 (£000)	19X2 (£000)	19X3 (£000)
Fixed assets	2,292	2,532	2,538	2,520
Goodwill	889	799	709	619
Current assets				
Stock	61	65	65	70
Debtors	1,965	2,118	2,464	2,715
ACT	–	11	47	47
	2,026	2,194	2,576	2,832
Current liabilities				
Creditors	1,067	852	946	1,053
VAT	130	182	237	263
Overdraft	1,138	1,006	1,475	893
Corporation Tax	260	252	387	431
HP balances*	–	580	950	1,215
	2,595	2,871	3,995	3,855
Net current assets/(liabilities)	(569)	(677)	(1,419)	(1,023)
Deferred taxation	(462)	(379)	(288)	(212)
Net assets	2,150	2,275	1,540	1,904
Share capital ordinary	220	220	220	220
preference	930	930	930	930
	1,150	1,150	1,150	1,150
Reserves	–	125	390	754
Loan	1,000	1,000	–	
	2,150	2,275	1,540	1,904

* Includes items due in more than one year.

Capital expenditure plans are an important issue for which detailed information is required at the financial preparation stage. A buy-out requiring substantial investment expenditure in addition to the servicing of a new financial structure may place an onerous burden on the funds generated from operations. A statement, such as that shown in Table 3.10, of fixed-asset movements and associated HP repayments, if any, helps identify areas which may give rise to concern.

Finally, the importance of the assumptions underlying the forecast statements was stressed earlier and in respect of MPF these

Table 3.10 Midlands Plating and Finishing Ltd: fixed assets

As at day one (1.1.19X1)	Cost	Depreciation	WDV	Depreciation rate %
Building improvements	336	–	336	10
Plant and machinery	3,828	2,012	1,816	20
Motor vehicles	110	29	81	25
Fixtures and fittings	93	34	59	10
	4,367	2,075	2,292	

Summary of forecast movements	Fixed-asset additions (£000)	Depreciation	HP repayments & deposits (£000)	HP interest charged in year (£000)
19X1	850	610	297	27
19X2	725	719	447	91
19X3	725	743	613	149

Table 3.11 Midlands Plating and Finishing Ltd: assumptions to forecasts

	19X1	19X2	19X3
Pension contributions	8.5%	8.5%	8.5%
Rate of inflation	6%	5%	4.5%
Wage increases (May)	6%	5%	4.5%
National Insurance contributions	8.5%	8.5%	8.5%
HP interest – flat	8%	8%	8%
Loan interest – flat	15%	15%	15%
Overdraft interest – flat	15%	15%	15%
Preference div 11.5% net	11.5%	11.5%	11.5%
Contingency (£000)	–	120	120
Debt-collection period – 53 days			
Overheads payment period (excluding salaries) – 60 days			

Note: Sales forecasts for the first half of 19X1 are based on current orders and customers' notifications. Sales forecasts thereafter are based on the directors' assessment of customers' requirements, having regard to trends within the industry and various other factors of which they are aware.

are summarised in Table 3.11. Management may expect to be asked to justify the basis of their assumptions.

Conclusions

The analyses and planning that we have discussed in this chapter and Chapter 2 are crucial in ensuring that the buy-out proposition gets to the starting gate. Should major problems of viability be highlighted in these stages, management have to find convincing solutions that would be put into practice after the buy-out and which they were unable to implement beforehand. Where convincing answers cannot be found, it may be wiser to accept that a buy-out is not possible rather than being carried away by enthusiasm in pursuing a hopeless venture.

CHAPTER 4

Raising the finance

Raising finance of the appropriate types and in the required quantities is a difficult task to be faced by managers buying out. Except in cases in the public eye, institutions are unlikely to beat a path to one's door, nor is it appropriate to approach every single institution that even hints at being active in the funding of management buy-outs. There exists what is to the unwary a bewildering array of types of finance available for buy-outs and an even larger number of institutions providing such funds. In explaining these different sources of funds, this chapter will emphasise the kind of approach that is required if the most appropriate financial package which fits a particular case is to be obtained.

Types of finance

The funding required to finance a management buy-out may be comprised of one type of funding, or perhaps four or five different and complementary elements. In order of increasing risk for the provider, the types of funds involved will typically include the following:

1. Clearing bank finance in the form of overdraft facilities, unsecured or more usually secured. Security is often obtained by either a fixed charge over a company's property and/or a floating charge over other assets. Where there are insufficient assets in the business to provide security, a personal guarantee from a director or a collateral charge/second mortgage on his/ her home may be sought. Charges and guarantees may take

various forms and it is necessary to be clear about the nature of these at the time of the buy-out. While it may be important for sufficient guarantees to be given to demonstrate personal commitment to a deal, overburdening management in this way may distract their full energies from running the business.

2.   Facilities from debt-factoring companies and other specialist providers of finance. Factoring essentially involves the sale of all or part of a company's debtor or receivables portfolio to the factor, who in return pays the cash value of the invoices, less service and interest charges. The advantage of factoring is that it can improve cash flow, particularly in fast-growing concerns with long and seasonal debtor payment cycles. In addition, for smaller companies, the service offered by factors of maintaining the debtor or receivables accounting records can obviate the need to install an in-house sales ledger function. Such benefits may well outweigh the often apparently high cost of the service.

3.   Loans. These can be secured or unsecured, at fixed or variable rates of interest (or with an option for either), with terms from a few months to 25 years, convertible into shares, with or without capital holidays and from banks or a variety of other financial institutions. In the field of management buy-outs the terms 'senior' and 'junior' debt are commonly used, signifying the relative ranking of the lenders in the event of a winding-up.

4.   Mezzanine debt. This term is often applied to debt that has equity characteristics – that is unsecured and therefore carrying an equity risk and commanding a higher rate of interest and often carrying rights to convert into equity, perhaps in the form of 'warrants'. The debt would be subordinated to all other forms of debt except normally (though not always) vendor loans and deferred consideration. As seen in Chapter 1, mezzanine debt has become a more significant element of the market from the late 1980s onwards.

5.   Vendor loans/deferred consideration. Loans made or simply an element of the purchase price deferred by the vendor to facilitate the financing of the buy-out. The rights attaching to this form of finance are as variable as those attaching to ordinary loans. Traditionally they have been interest free and subordinate to all other debt, although frequently they carried a right, reducing over the period of repayment, to participate in shareholders' profits in the event of the sale of shares.

6. Preference shares. Again, preference shares can come in as wide a variety as loans, except that they cannot be secured on any of the company's assets. Classified generally as equity they usually have no equity voting rights except in exceptional circumstances (such as a failure to pay a dividend or make a redemption). In practice they are used as another means by which management's share of equity can be geared up. In terms of income their advantage is that they have a servicing cost only if the company is profitable and furthermore that cost is charged as an appropriation of profit, not as a charge on profits.
7. Equity share capital provided by the buy-out team and financing institutions. The equity share capital is itself usually divided into different rights and priority on a winding up (the management team often ending up as the only class holding straight ordinary shares ranking last of all). The different rights for institutional investors are designed to give the institutions, as minority holders of shares, protection which would not be available to them as straight ordinary shareholders.

Traditionally, the required capital structure for a buy-out is evolved by calculating, perhaps in collaboration with a banker, the extent to which bank facilities can be used to provide the finance required. This identifies the 'financing gap', and it is in respect of this that the team will have to turn to providers of risk capital, such as venture and development capital institutions and BES funds. In some buy-outs, the subsequent sale of assets which are surplus to requirements may contribute a significant element of the requisite finance and may, indeed, be looked for as a form of insurance by financing institutions. Increasingly bankers are prepared to lend not just specifically against assets but also on the strength of predictable cash flows. Accordingly it is not always appropriate to adopt this 'bottom-up' approach to structuring although it remains a good starting point for most buy-outs and buy-ins.

The structure of the finance package and the use of the various types of finance depend partly upon the kind of buy-out and partly upon the idiosyncracies of the financing institution. Whatever structure is arrived at, it is necessary to assess carefully the ability of the business to service and repay any loan elements as well as to provide an adequate return for equity and quasi-equity holders.

In some cases, more often in the smaller buy-outs, it may be possible to fund the purchase entirely from the personal resources of the management team, who may acquire all the ordinary share capital, and from a bank loan and/or overdraft facility. Generally speaking, however, the larger the buy-out, the lower will be management's percentage share of the equity (because of their limited resources), the more financing institutions that will be involved and the more complex will be the mix of the funding types that are used. In the very large buy-outs, several layers of finance may be used. For example, a financing package may include a bank term loan with a floating interest rate (senior bank debt); an element of high-coupon fixed-interest loan stock ranking after the banks but before equity (mezzanine or intermediate finance), with the intermediate lender taking part of the equity but being willing to accept a lower overall rate of return in exchange for greater security; and an equity layer with management funding ordinary shares and financing institutions a mixture of equity, preference shares and possibly unsecured loan stock.

More specific aspects of financial structure, together with a worked example, will be discussed in Chapter 5.

Sources of finance

One of the most remarkable business phenomena in the United Kingdom in the 1980s has been the growth in the number of venture and development capital investing institutions interested in financing MBOs (see for example the institutions included in *The Economist Guide to Management Buy-outs* and the *UK Venture Capital Journal*, published by Venture Economics). This growth has already been discussed in detail in Chapter 1. Prior to this explosion, the principal source of capital for such transactions was derived from 3i (Investors in Industry), together with a small number of other well-established institutions. As management buy-outs became more familiar, an increasing number of venture and development capital institutions set out their stalls as being willing and able to finance and assist buy-outs. There are over 100 institutions in the UK which so describe themselves.

The volume of the potential sources of finance can be both daunting and confusing for the potential MBO team. It is helpful, therefore, to try to identify the principal types of fund and to differentiate their objectives, thus helping potential MBO teams to establish both their own funding options and the most appropriate source of finance.

It is vitally important to recognise at the outset that financial institutions are not just sources of money. When they invest, there is a sort of marriage. If the partners have compatible aims and objectives, or indeed if there is an element of constructive tension in the relationship, both parties can benefit. If there is a total mismatch, the consequences can be financially damaging to the investor and sometimes disastrous for the management buy-out team, who do not usually get a second chance.

It is possible to draw a distinction between those institutions which subscribe only equity or other forms of share capital, and those which can provide loan finance as well. A further difference arises through the maximum and minimum size of investment a particular institution may be prepared to make. In general, the venture capital arms of the clearing banks are able to offer a full package of equity and debt-related finance.

Traditionally, 3i has been prepared to invest for the long term, although it has always been happy to disinvest at a sufficiently attractive price should the opportunity arise. The sheer magnitude of the 3i operation has inevitably meant that many of its practices and methods have been widely copied elsewhere. To some extent, this strategy has been a function of the size of investment: 3i has always made investments in relatively small businesses, sometimes placing only a few thousand pounds. It is unlikely (although not unknown) that such investments will grow sufficiently to obtain a listing, and a sale might not be acceptable to the management. Therefore the return on investment is likely to be through dividends. The rate of dividend required on such small investments is likely to be quite high, reflecting both the disproportionately high costs of initial appraisal and monitoring, and the inherent risk attaching to a very small or young company.

Apart from the clearing banks, few other institutions (see Chapter 1) are prepared to invest such small amounts as 3i, and few see themselves as obtaining their reward so much from dividend flow. A more typical investing institution would have a minimum investment of perhaps £500,000 and some participation in profits through dividends on a formula basis, and would expect an 'exit' – i.e. the opportunity to realise its investment either via a trade sale or flotation – within three to five years. Such an institution might be prepared to invest on its own account several million pounds and would be prepared to participate in, and possibly lead, syndicates for much larger sums. The principal objective of such an institution will be capital gain and, dependent upon the profile of the business in which the investment is to be made, it may well be possible to avoid any running yield at all – other than, perhaps, a management fee or the fees of a non-executive director. The entry into the UK market of US-based institutions has seen more emphasis on loan financing for larger buy-outs, with exit sought through loan repayment rather than Stock Exchange listing.

Since the management buy-out market continues to develop rapidly, and the preferences of the institutions also change in terms of both the industry and size of clients and funding preferences (types of finance, syndication or not, etc.), it is not appropriate to provide further details of specific institutions here. Interested readers are referred to the publications cited at the beginning of this section. It is useful, however, to discuss general principles of approaching an institution.

Finding and approaching the right institution

The key to finding the right institution is the correct identification of the strengths, weaknesses and true potential (or lack of it) of the business contemplating the buy-out, and matching the requirements of the business with those of the institution. Such an objective assessment is extremely difficult for the individuals forming the team to make. People who work hard in, and have a commitment to, a particular business can often see its potential but do not recognise the changes needed, frequently within the management team, to realise that potential. They may see the market for their new products or services but be unaware of parallel developments taking place in their competitors.

The initial approach of an MBO team to the institution(s) of their choice will usually be supported by a proposal, the preparation and contents of which have been discussed in Chapter 3. Such a proposal arriving on an institution's desk normally has only one chance to be considered. It is, therefore, vital that it meets the standard the institution will expect, particularly in terms of objectivity and credibility. If it does not, the chance to get the right institution involved may well be lost.

The larger institutions receive many hundreds of proposals for funding from all sorts of businesses in a year. Their knowledge of any one of the industries in which such businesses operate is likely to be superficial compared with that of operators within that industry, but they *will* have the advantage of an overview, and the opportunity to make comparisons. The comparison will take account of the clarity and logic of the proposal, the credibility of the business plan and, as a corollary, of the perceived quality of management.

Because of the critical nature of this first approach, it is highly desirable that proper professional advice is taken at an early stage. This will normally mean contacting one of the relatively few firms of accountants or lawyers that have expertise and a reputation in this area.

The role of such a professional, in the early stages of formulating a buy-out proposal, is primarily to advise on the viability of the outline proposal, on how and from where the necessary funding could be obtained and on the best means of opening and conducting negotiations with the prospective vendor and with the financier. Perhaps, most important of all, he can give the team a 'dry run' – an opportunity to rehearse and to be challenged on their plans, motivation and, indeed, competence before the crucial meetings with institutions.

Some institutions, particularly in the larger transactions, will take over the team's negotiations without necessarily involving external professionals, and will themselves conduct negotiations with the vendors. They will 'deliver the deal'.

This option may be attractive to the team. It provides 'one-stop shopping'. The backing of a major financial institution may well assist significantly in the negotiations with the vendor, giving credibility and a strong negotiating position to the team. However, it has the disadvantage that such an institution is acting both as adviser and provider of funds for the team. The opportunity for the team to test the market in relation to the funds being provided to them, for the cost of funding, or in respect of the size of their equity stake, is lost. For this reason it is always advisable for the team to retain its own professional adviser; indeed, many of the institutions in the market will strongly advise the team to do so.

As has already been indicated, the financial institutions providing funds for buy-outs have a variety of investment objectives, are interested in investing different sums of money, and seek to achieve their investment returns in different ways and over varying periods. Further, some institutions have a special interest and expertise in certain industries, notably in high technology or in businesses at a particular phase of development. Matching the requirements of the business to be bought out with the right institution requires some skill and knowledge of the market. The practice adopted by some teams and by some of the less-experienced advisers in sending out standard-format proposals to some 20 or 30 institutions is ineffective and damaging to the teams' interests. It is unpopular with institutions that like to be treated on an individual basis, and, since institutions are in contact with each other regularly and informally, it rapidly becomes apparent that the approach is far from selective. A rejection from one institution may well trigger rejection from all.

The best method of approach is, therefore, to develop, in conjunction with an appropriate professional, a succinct but comprehensive proposal based on the business plan as discussed in Chapter 3. This should give the addressees a clear view of what the business does; what its recent performance has been; what can reasonably be expected in the future based on a cogent appraisal of market competition, products, management structure, skills and past record; and what funding is required. Summaries of financial performance in the recent past and of projections for the future must be included. The proposal should be neither so bulky that it intimidates or bores the recipient, nor so abbreviated that it begs too many questions or appears superficial.

Once such a proposal has been prepared, with a greater or lesser degree of assistance from advisers, an initial approach should be made to financial institutions whose investment objectives are compatible with those set out in the proposal. Often this first contact will be made by the adviser on an informal basis to find out whether the proposal is likely to be of interest to the selected institution. If the response is positive, a copy of the proposal will be sent out, perhaps to four such institutions to enable an assessment to be made of the market perception of the proposal and of the terms which can be negotiated for the provision of finance. At this time it is also usual to make contact with one or more clearing banks to discuss with them the provision of bank finance. They will normally be given a slightly abridged version of the proposal with, perhaps, some additional material addressing the areas of particular interest to them, such as details of the assets available as security.

The next stage in raising the finance is likely to absorb a great deal of the management's time. Once the institutions and the bankers have indicated an interest in principle, they will want to meet the management, to tour locations and, quite probably, to speak to customers and possibly suppliers. Since at this stage there may well be three venture or development capital houses, two clearing banks and perhaps leasing companies involved, senior management may become extremely harassed and possibly dis-enchanted, and there is the real danger that the day-to-day operations of the business may be prejudiced. However, since the terms offered by both institutions and bankers can vary quite widely, and because there is usually a considerable element of uncertainty about whether a particular institution will make an offer until quite a late stage, such apparent proliferation of potential financiers is normally not merely desirable but essential.

Following the initial visits and appraisals the attitudes of the institutions will become clearer. Some may feel, to use a phrase much loved in the industry, that the investment is 'not for us'. Others may wish to proceed to the next stage. Practice varies between institutions. Some may at this stage be able to make an offer, subject to contract and to an accountants' investigation or to other conditions; others may not be prepared to make any offer until investigation procedures are completed. It is at this time that the decision usually has to be made about which institution is to be proceeded with, because it is now that significant costs are likely to start being incurred through the employment of the investigating accountants. Again, the advice of the professional adviser can be most important, because he may well be able, through his informal contacts with the institutions, to form a fairly clear view of the extent of commitment to invest by the competing financiers. Nevertheless, this remains a delicate period.

Conclusions

There is a bewildering array of financial sources for buy-outs, in terms of both the types of finance and the institutions providing them. It is essential for the management attempting to buy out to appreciate that institutions see a great number of buy-out proposals and that it is necessary to present to them a clear and objective assessment of the business. Moreover, it is necessary to identify and convince the financier who will best satisfy the buy-out's needs, without hawking the proposal endlessly around innumerable institutions. Professional advisers can economise on this search procedure, enabling management to devote at least some of their energies to keeping the business running.

In the end, it will be discovered that when taken to extremes finance is a commodity like any other. The difference is that an investing institution can be an asset to a business or it can be a burden and which category it falls into depends on the outlook and philosophy of the institution as expressed by its directors and staff.

This personal chemistry is often the determining factor in the matching of a buy-out and its principal funder.

The detailed considerations affecting the structure of the financial package and the conduct of the whole buy-out transaction are dealt with in the next three chapters.

CHAPTER 5

Structuring the financial package

Management buy-outs have often been referred to as the way to acquire a business with other people's money. The problem is that lenders tend to want their money back, plus a return for their trouble. If management are also to obtain a financial reward that adequately reflects their efforts and taking of risks, it is important to structure the financial package with great care.

The starting point is the price to be paid, which determines the total amount of finance required. Being able to negotiate as fair a price as possible helps improve the degree of flexibility in financing and ultimately the size of the equity stake that management obtain. In general, the structure of the financing package requires a balance to be found between the amount of debt and non-debt finance, in a way which enables the purchase price to be funded without undue risk of bankruptcy and which gives management a sufficient equity stake to ensure a high level of incentive. How management are to find their contribution and eventually repay any borrowings they may need to make in the process is also an important ingredient in structuring the overall package. These issues are now dealt with in detail.

Price

No more important decision will be made in the course of the buy-out than that of the price at which the business can be bought. The implications of that decision will have a fundamental bearing on the health of the business after the buy-out and, indeed, may well be the key factor in determining whether or not it survives.

The price at which a buy-out can occur is subject to one major constraint that is not present when, for example, one established company acquires another. In the latter case, too high a price paid may be damaging but the profit and cash flows derived from the existing business of the purchaser can, in most cases, effectively subsidise any inadequacy of return from the business which has been purchased.

This comfort or fall-back does not apply to a management buy-out. In essence, the purchase price paid in a buy-out has to be funded and ultimately repaid out of the cash generated by the business in the period after the buy-out. If the business is to survive and prosper it will probably require a substantial proportion of the cash flow which it generates from trading to finance its own working capital expansion and capital expenditure. Thus it is only what might be termed the 'excess' or 'free' cash flow which is available to fund the buy-out cost.

Since this constraint is so fundamental, its implications must be addressed at an early stage in considering the feasibility of a buy-out. Once the cash flow projections associated with the business plan and the proposal have been prepared and allowance made for contingencies, it will be possible to identify the amount of the net cash generated available to service debt taken on as part of the funding of the buy-out – to pay dividends on preference or participating shares and ultimately to repay debt or redeem preference shares. This net available cash effectively sets the top level to the price at which the purchase can be completed, and the team must reconcile themselves to the prospect of not proceeding if it proves impossible to negotiate a price below this limit. The consequences of paying too much can be catastrophic.

Of course, negotiation on price with the vendor would not normally start at the maximum price payable. The commercial factors affecting what the team should offer and the vendor accept will obviously be different in each case. The factors which influence the value placed on the business by vendors, management and competing external bidders have been analysed in Table 2.4. Of particular importance here are the following:
1. The business to be bought out or the characteristics of its management may be such that it is difficult for the vendor to sell to anyone other than the incumbent management. This situation arises quite frequently in specialist service companies or companies where the personal skills or reputation of the' management in the market are the main strengths of the

company. If such management were to leave to join a competitor or to set up their own business in competition, the value of the company to the vendor would be very limited. Although the vendor might not at first recognise or accept it, the management are in a very good negotiating position in such a case.

2. A second factor to consider is whether there are any pressures on the vendor to sell, either from external sources as a consequence of financial difficulties, or internally in relation, perhaps, to a partially implemented strategic change to which continued ownership of the potential buy-out company is an obstruction or irritant.

3. An attempt should always be made to ascertain the price at which the vendor can afford to sell. Many factors will affect this, particularly in the case of US and European parents – which seem to have a very marked reluctance to dispose of any subsidiary, even under duress, at less than 'book value'. This can effectively stop a buy-out if the projected return on such 'book value' is inadequate for buy-out funding purposes.

4. Where the potential buy-out company is a significant element of a listed group, it is also unlikely that a sale can be achieved at a price which represents a price/earnings ratio lower than that enjoyed by the vendor.

In addition to considering such factors directly affecting the vendor, the buy-out team should research what the fair price for their business might be, by reference to the share prices of listed competitors or similar companies, or to recent sales of such companies. Part of the professional adviser's role, and indeed that of the prospective financiers, is to advise on the fair price and to assist in the negotiations to achieve that price.

The mechanics of the financial structure

Initial considerations

It was suggested in Chapter 4 that the construction of an appropriate financial structure to enable the agreed price to be paid should start with identifying that part of the total funding which can be met from clearing-bank facilities or from other providers of debt.

The principal reason for tackling the problem in this manner is that the greater the proportion of the total funding which can be provided in the form of debt, the smaller the amount of fixed capital that is required. Since management are usually restricted in the amount of fixed capital they can provide from personal sources, the less the *total* fixed capital required, the greater will be the management's share of the whole equity of the business.

A second and closely related argument for a highly geared funding structure is the effect on the value of equity of enhanced profitability, where gearing is high. Once the admittedly high fixed costs of servicing the large debt burdens are covered, profit accrues at a high rate to the small capital base, producing a very fast growth in value. On the other hand, there is a corresponding increase in risk. If profits do not cover the high interest costs, the business is in serious trouble and may fail. There are, however, at least two fundamental constraints on the amount of debt that can be built into the financial structure of a buy-out. First, lenders will apply their own disciplines and limits to the total borrowing in any one case. Secondly, venture and development capital institutions providing equity funds will almost certainly seek to restrict borrowings. Concern has been expressed on both sides of the Atlantic about the stability of large very highly geared buy-outs, and the UK financial establishment seems to be taking a conservative and probably prudent view of what is an acceptable degree of leverage. This problem may be exacerbated where apparent 'free' cash flows are either not as stable as expected or not really free, i.e. they may be required to take care of investment needs or to take account of new investment opportunities.

While a significant proportion of equity capital continues to feature in most buy-outs, the leveraged buy-out is increasingly common among larger deals and, perhaps not surprisingly, in buy-outs of public companies. The lenders will tend to regard these larger transactions as more secure and capable of significant cash generation. Recent experience suggests, however that such assumptions cannot be applied universally. Ironically it is the retail sector, which because of its strong cash flow has been the most popular for larger management buy-outs and buy-ins, that has illustrated this vulnerability most publicly. What has tended to be overlooked is that the retail sector has traditionally been highly vulnerable to cyclical downturns.

Clearing-bank facilities

The limitations on total borrowings approved by banks will be derived largely from an assessment of the extent of available appropriate security and an appraisal of the strength and stability of the income flow supporting the debt service cost.

Bankers will usually look to trade debtors as their primary security for overdraft facilities. Typically, a clearing bank might be prepared to advance between 60 per cent and 70 per cent of good trade debtors on a secured basis if all other factors were satisfactory. Further facilities may be available, secured on other specific assets such as premises and major plant items, again subject to total borrowing levels and interest cover being satisfactory.

Bank overdraft facilities made available for working-capital requirements are, theoretically at least, repayable on demand, and should be self-liquidating. Bankers like to see customer accounts swinging in and out of credit. While the practice frequently differs from this ideal, it is prudent, in creating the financing structure for a buy-out, to try to achieve a proper banking structure – for the very good reason that properly constructed and operated facilities are likely to offer more scope for flexibility, should a problem arise, than an already abused overdraft facility.

Accordingly, where substantial bank facilities are going to be required for a significant period in relation to the buy-out, it is probably advisable to fund them as a term loan with a specific repayment schedule, and to use the overdraft in a proper manner. The goodwill of the banker and the credibility of the management team in his eyes are important elements in the safe operation of most companies following a buy-out.

Other debt-related funding

An alternative to the use of clearing-bank facilities secured on debtors is to use a credit factoring line from a specialist factoring institution. The attraction here for a small company is that the factoring house can usually, if required, provide an accounting and administration service for trade debtors. An advantage for both the smaller and large business is that advances can amount to between 70 per cent and 80 per cent of trade debtors, considerably greater than those normally available from clearing banks on overdraft.

A widely used alternative source of finance in constructing a buy-out is leasing, either in respect of new capital spending after the buy-out – thus releasing cash to assist the repayment of the funding needed to buy the business – or as part of the original buy-out funding, through a sale and leaseback scheme. This latter route is quite extensively used for vehicle fleets, and sometimes for plant. However, it is less likely to be of use for property because the covenant of the newly bought-out business may not be sufficiently attractive to institutions in this market.

A third element sometimes used in funding buy-outs is an unsecured loan, unsecured loan stock or possibly convertible unsecured loan stock. These are probably of greater use in large buy-outs than in small, where the degree of risk may make them very unattractive to the creditor or loan stock holder. They can, however, be a useful device where subscription for a similar amount as risk capital would dilute the management's stake to such an extent as to demotivate them, or as a more tax-efficient alternative to redeemable preference share. Such unsecured lending would fall into the category now commonly described as mezzanine (see Chapter 4).

Fixed capital
This general description covers equity, quasi-equity and redeemable shares. Previous paragraphs have discussed the principle of debt finance in 'leveraging' the total funding, and the types of debt-related funding usually available in devising the financial structure of a buy-out. It is now appropriate to consider what influences the decision on how much of the total funding should be in the form of fixed capital, and the form such capital should take.

It is a long-established accounting principle that share capital should buy the fixed assets of a business, and make a contribution to the funding of working capital. While this principle owes its origins to manufacturing industry many years ago, it is still a perfectly sound point from which to start creating the financial structure.

Having said that, the principle is clearly at odds with two interrelated factors affecting buy-outs. First, in some industries it may imply a very substantial capital base in relation to the overall size of the business. If the management are severely restricted in the total share capital for which they can subscribe, this may result in their having an unreasonably small stake in the business. Secondly, it may imply a relatively low level of borrowing which, while it may produce a secure business, is likely to produce a distinctly unexciting growth in value either for the institution which subscribed equity or for the management.

In practice the relationship between fixed capital and debt in any buy-out is a matter of judgement in each particular case, taking account of the matters discussed above, the risk element in the forecasts, the level of projected capital expenditure, the demand for working capital and the availability of suitable assets to provide security for lenders. By intelligent use of different types of fixed capital it may be possible to combine both the benefit of a large capital base and, effectively, some leverage on what might be called the 'core' shares. The example in Table 5.1 illustrates the point.

This funding was arranged for a buy-out where the total amount required at completion was £4,250,000, giving a safety margin of some £600,000 for growth in working capital. The example shows how the management have obtained 40 per cent of a substantial business for £150,000. In this case leverage is provided by the use of redeemable preference shares and the unsecured loan and although this has had a material adverse effect on the apparent capital gearing the profitability and positive cash flow of the business gives ample cover for the interest charge.

A further factor worth mentioning in the example is the phasing of the repayments of the medium-term loan and redeemable preference shares. Great care was taken at the planning stage to analyse the profile of the foreseeable cash generation. As a consequence, negotiations ensured that the medium-term loan was repayable by equal instalments over four years commencing at the first anniversary of the buy-out, with the preference shares to be redeemed in years six to ten.

It is also interesting to note that the combined tangible and intangible fixed assets in this buy-out amounted to £3,600,000. It was neither possible nor, indeed, commercially justified to match this figure with fixed capital, but the total share capital, together with the mezzanine loan and the specifically secured medium-term loan, equates closely to this figure, and thus the relationship between long-term assets and long-term liabilities was preserved.

Table 5.1 Example of financial structure

	%	£
Share capital		
Management team (ordinary)	40	150,000
Institution (participating ordinary)	60	225,000
	100	375,000
Redeemable preference shares		750,000
Shareholders' funds		1,125,000
Unsecured mezzanine loan		1,000,000
Medium-term loan (secured on properties and other specific assets)		1,450,000
Overdraft facilities		1,300,000
Total funding		£4,875,000

The example dealt with a relatively substantial company with an established profitable trade and plenty of assets to provide security. Where, as is often the case with service-industry companies, there are insignificant fixed assets, devising an appropriate funding structure and obtaining the necessary support can prove quite difficult. Since there are few assets to provide security, any package is likely to contain a large element of risk capital. However, this arrangement will tend to reduce the proportion of the managers' equity following the buy-out, in a business which probably relies very heavily on those managers' talents. Such managers commonly feel that they are being asked to pay a high price for an adequate stake in the business which, in many cases, they have been responsible for building up. A few years ago this was seen as a rather intractable problem, and it was felt to be difficult to achieve a buy-out of such a business.

There is still no perfect answer, but increasing sophistication in capital structures has resulted in buy-outs of this type of company being readily achievable on terms acceptable to their management. Again, each case has to be considered on an individual basis, but there are some common elements.

The objective must be to reconcile the requirement of the management to have a relatively large stake in the business with the institution's requirement for a high reward for what is seen as a high-risk investment. This can be achieved by the use of what is known as a 'ratchet'. The mechanics can vary but, in essence, the management attain a higher proportion of the equity in the bought-out business the better the business performs, within certain parameters. For example, the management might have 40 per cent of a bought-out consulting company at completion. If the average profits over the first two years exceed (say) £400,000 but are under £450,000, management achieve 44 per cent of the total equity. If profits on the basis agreed between the parties exceed £450,000, management achieve 48 per cent. There might also be an adverse adjustment if profits were to fall below another predetermined figure. Ratchets can also be based upon the market capitalisation achieved by the company on flotation or sale or simply on the internal rate of return achieved by the institution (with the speed of loan repayment therefore becoming a critical element of such a calculation) with an agreed valuation formula in the event that the company is not sold or floated or on achievement of certain funding repayment targets. Negotiating such a ratchet can be difficult and the documentation can be complex but, at best, it can provide a mechanism which motivates management to achieve good results and enhances the financial rewards of both management and financiers. At worst, a ratchet mechanism can result in a protracted dispute between the two parties which adversely affects the operations of the business. Such a dispute can arise because of capital expenditure plans which have a short-term depressive effect on results in a crucial year, because stock-market conditions do not favour a flotation, because inflation has distorted the figures on which the ratchet was premised, because taxation rates have changed – any number of reasons why financiers generally prefer not to use them. They survive however because of competitive pressure amongst financiers to make investments.

Implications of the financial structure on the team

The implications of participating in a management buy-out often seem extremely daunting to individual managers. Initially there is usually a lack of understanding of how they, with their relatively modest resources, can raise sufficient funds to buy their business. Once the scheme has been constructed there is usually such pressure to complete the acquisition that the personal funding aspects tend to be dealt with in haste and at a late stage.

The average personal financial contribution by each member of a management team appears to be between £20,000 and £40,000. For a typical UK salaried employee this represents a substantial commitment, and one which is normally made only by recourse to bank loans, usually secured on the family home. Both the individuals and the bankers are frequently concerned about how such sums are to be serviced and ultimately repaid.

Broadly speaking under present UK tax law, interest paid by a member of a buy-out team to enable him to buy shares in what is defined for tax purposes as a 'close' company is allowed as a deduction against the individual's other income for tax purposes. If, as is frequently the case, the individual's income is already fully committed, it will be necessary to increase his remuneration following the buy-out sufficiently to enable him to pay the interest. Since the interest is tax-deductible, remuneration need only be increased by the net after-tax amount, but this increase in remuneration must be built into the cash-flow forecasts included in the proposal sent to institutions. It is also important to check that the detailed offer of funds from the financial institution, which frequently includes a restriction on directors' remuneration after the buy-out, does not conflict with the need to pay this increased remuneration.

In buy-outs where the team is large, or where there are several financiers involved, the bought-out company may not be 'close'. In these cases taxation relief will not be available on the team's borrowings, and the additional remuneration will be correspondingly increased. It is important to determine the tax status of the new company at an early stage for this reason.

In any event tax law is so complex and so susceptible to change that management teams should tread with extreme care, taking professional advice whenever decisions are taken on the assumption of a particular tax treatment.

While the problems of servicing the personal debt burden are usually relatively easily overcome, the question of repayment is much more intractable. In larger buy-outs, where a Stock Exchange listing or an Unlisted Securities quotation is anticipated in the foreseeable future, the problem can probably be resolved by repaying borrowings from the proceeds of the sale of some shares at that date. Even in this case, however, there is a significant element of uncertainty. The company might not make its forecasts, or the market conditions might make it wholly inappropriate to seek a public quotation. In smaller cases there is, realistically, only the prospect of an outright sale of the business and, possibly, of the company buying back its own shares to provide the necessary capital sum. This latter option is, in any event, likely to be significantly delayed if there are institutional equity investors in the company as well, because such investors will almost certainly require to be bought out first, and the company's cash resources are unlikely to be able to deal with more than a limited volume of share purchases in a financial period.

One option is to pay remuneration sufficient to enable the recipients to repay their borrowings, although this may require a very substantial charge against profits to produce a significant net sum in the hands of the recipient. Thus a director whose top tax rate is 40 per cent will need additional gross remuneration of over £8,000 to enable him to repay borrowings of £5,000. If there are a number of such directors, the effect on the distributable profits of the company in any one year is considerable.

A solution which is possible in some cases, but not all, is to use a directors' pension scheme as collateral (although no formal charge can be created) for an ultimate repayment out of the tax-free lump sum on retirement. The legal and taxation implications of such a scheme need careful review. It may not be attractive where the management team are relatively young, in which case the repayment of the borrowings will be deferred for an excessively long period after the buy-out, and the existence of large borrowings may restrict house purchases and other domestic arrangements. In such cases, it is more usual to repay the borrowings gradually out of enhanced income, or to secure a sale of some shares to a third party at some future date. (Exit routes are addressed in Chapter 8.)

Where no external equity investor is involved in the buy-out, i.e., where all external funding has been in the form of debt, it may be possible to provide for the ultimate repayment of the management team's borrowings by subscribing a proportion of their capital as redeemable shares, or as deferred loan capital, if overall gearing levels permit. For example, if the total management stake in a buy-out is £120,000 and all other funding is in the form of debt, it might be possible to subscribe (say) £10,000 in ordinary share capital and £110,000 as redeemable preference shares. Obviously, the lenders would wish to ensure that the preference shares were not repaid out of funding which they had subscribed, or in advance of repayment of their loans, and the shares could not be redeemed until the financial resources of the company were adequate. Nevertheless, such an arrangement can provide a simple mechanism for putting the management in funds to repay their personal borrowings, without adverse taxation effects.

Financial controls

Much has already been said in this book about the need for careful planning and forecasting in the preparation of a management buy-out. Almost any business is commercially and financially vulnerable following a buy-out. Competitors may well see an opportunity to attack in the market-place, suppliers may restrict credit, the financiers will be at maximum exposure and understandably nervous. It is likely that a condition of the offer of finance will have been the provision of regular financial information. Failure to provide such information, or worse still an unpleasant surprise, will damage the business or its managers' credibility severely. It is sad but true that almost all surprises in business are unpleasant.

It is absolutely vital that the financial and commercial aspects of the business are under tight and effective control, that objectives are clearly understood, and that there are contingency plans developed and ready to be implemented if things start to go wrong.

As any receiver will confirm, the most common single contributory factor in company failures is lack of information about what is happening to the business. In a post-buy-out situation, the absolute priority is accurate, timely and relevant financial information. The most critical of all areas is cash management. If this is to be achieved there must be totally reliable data, effective credit control and tight controls over purchase authorisation and buying policy, together with the necessary technical skills to produce, flex and roll forward cash forecasts. In small businesses much of the control will be directly in the hands of the management, but there may well be inadequate technical skills continually to update cash forecasts. In such cases, management would be wise to enlist professional help on a regular basis to prepare and update cash forecasts and probably to help in producing other financial information as well.

In larger businesses the problem may be somewhat different. There may well be established accounting and control systems, and substantial financial and technical expertise. But very often some key areas of the overall financial management of the company have been carried out, before the buy-out, elsewhere in the group. There may be a gap in the system after the buy-out which is not immediately recognised by the management. As part of the planning for the buy-out it is essential, therefore, for businesses of all sizes to review their present management and financial information systems and to make such changes as will enable them to obtain, both for internal management purposes and for reporting to external financiers, prompt and accurate financial data on achieved performance, and sufficiently detailed and reliable data to enable forecasting and budgeting to be carried out as a routine management tool. Again, the advice of professional accountants is very desirable, and is frequently insisted upon by financiers.

Conclusions

Clearly, the structuring of the financial package is a crucial element in the future success of the buy-out.

The applicability of the various options available to a particular buy-out depends on the circumstances of the case and on the preferences of different institutions. Although it is possible to restructure the financial package after the buy-out in order to take account of new investment opportunities, or if events do not turn out as expected, it is preferable to adopt from the start an appropriate package for the business which will, as far as possible, allow unforeseen developments to be accommodated.

CHAPTER 6

Implementing a buy-out

In Chapter 4 much emphasis was put upon the need to produce a proposal which is succinct yet comprehensive, and sufficiently interesting and credible to attract attention from financial institutions. This chapter will look in a little greater detail at the work which both professional advisers and financiers will do in vetting proposals and carrying out what is known as due diligence, and will then consider some of the practical aspects of implementing the buy-out.

The proposal and the role of advisers

The proposal submitted to institutions will normally contain an overview of the proposal, a brief section on the history and present business of the company, details of the management team, a description of the products or services, production and other facilities, markets, competition, managements' objectives and a financial section. This last section should contain actual financial results for the last three years, profit forecasts and cash-flow forecasts, probably for one year in detail and two in outline, projected balance sheets at completion and at the next three accounting period ends, and the main assumptions adopted by the management in preparing the financial information. (See Chapter 3 for full discussion.)

The proposal as a whole will be subject to careful scrutiny by the institutions and will form the starting point for their own 'due diligence', i.e., work they carry out to corroborate and amplify the information in the proposal to supplement their own authorisation procedures. Obviously, what emerges as a consequence of the due-diligence work will have a crucial effect on management's credibility, and hence on the chances of the deal proceeding.

If, as was suggested in Chapter 4, the team appoint professional accountants as advisers prior to submitting a proposal to an institution, they will have an opportunity to test the validity of the proposal as informed outsiders before seeing institutions, and such advisers will carry out their own appraisal before recommending the proposal to institutions.

The total vetting procedure will scrutinise some or all of the issues covered in Chapter 3, as follows:

1. **Management.** Prior references may well be sought and details of CVs checked since institutions, which are largely backing the management, require as much certainty as possible that individuals have achieved what they claim and do not have any 'skeletons in the cupboard'.

2. **Products, markets and competition.** In larger cases where the company has an established product or service, trade sources will be checked to ensure that the product or service is satisfactory, that it is well received by customers and that it is competitive. It may be that a limited market research programme will be carried out or, possibly, an economic survey. Publicity material in relation to the company, its competition and its industry will also be reviewed.

3. **Production or other facilities.** Facilities will be inspected and it is probable that a consultant with knowledge of the characteristics of the industry will be employed to report on the adequacy and efficiency of the installation and systems.

4. **Financial data.** All the financial appendices will be scrutinised for compatibility with recent actual financial performance and with the objectives defined by management. Findings arising from a review of the market opportunities will also be compared with the financial projections. Additionally, a financially orientated review will be carried out either internally by the institution or by an independent firm of chartered accountants.

The financial investigation will normally cover the following:

- a detailed review of trading performance over the previous three accounting periods;
- a review of the profit and cash-flow projections and the underlying assumptions;
- consideration of the adequacy of the proposed funding for the future requirements of the business;

- an appraisal of management and accounting control of the business.

It is also usual for the reporting accountants to give an informed and often oral report to the institution on the adequacy of management performance and cover.

The accountants' report will highlight areas of recent trading performance which are of an abnormal nature, or which are likely to have an effect, whether positive or negative, on the projected results. They will also review the assumptions used in the forecasts to see whether they are compatible with the experience of the company in the recent past, and whether they are reasonable in the light of the economic or business circumstances prevailing at the time of the report.

For example, it may be that two assumptions in respect of the cash-flow forecasts are that trade debtors will be collected within an average of 60 days from the date of sale, and that bank base rates will be 10.5 per cent. If a review of recent practice indicates that debtor collection periods average 70 days and that base rates are 12.5 per cent, both matters will be reported upon, since they will have a significant impact on the funding required.

One of the advantages of appointing accountants as advisers at an early stage is that they will carry out an initial review of most of the aspects to be covered by the financial investigation and will usually be able to identify points of weakness within the proposal. This enables management to make any amendments necessary to the plan or to develop a rational explanation for any apparent illogicalities or variations in trends without the risk of damaging credibility and possibly causing the buy-out to be aborted.

As will be obvious, the whole 'due diligence' procedure will require considerable commitment of time from senior managers of the company, who have to be on hand to answer questions, show various investigators round, and to agree the factual content of the independent accountants' report. It is usual for tempers to get frayed at this stage and for management to feel that they are inundated with expensive professional advisers and are having their attention distracted from running the business. All this is perfectly true but, in larger cases in particular, unavoidable. It is therefore very important that, at the early stage of implementation, management are aware of the potentially disruptive effect of the various investigations and take steps to minimise the potential problems. One way of dealing with this problem is, where possible, for part of the management team to handle the buy-out, with the rest concentrating on running the business.

Negotiations with the vendor

General

Chapter 5 discussed some of the factors that will determine the price to be paid for the business. It is obviously important that the likelihood of the management buy-out proceeding at a price which can be afforded is established at as early a stage as possible. If this is not done, a great deal of time will probably have been wasted and the management team may well have incurred significant professional costs.

Determining the sequence in which the various matters which are involved in a buy-out should occur, and the precise time when an offer should be made, are two of the more difficult decisions that have to be made. There is a real dilemma here: it is unwise to make an offer without reasonable expectation that it can be supported by appropriate funding, yet it is difficult and imprudent to try to create a funding structure on a price basis which is unrealistic. Whatever happens, once an offer is made relations between management and the vendor can never be the same again.

There is no universal solution to this problem, but there are some generally applicable solutions. As discussed in Chapter 5, the maximum price which can be paid in a buy-out is determined by the internal cash generation of the company. It follows, therefore, that the first stage must always be to prepare and assess the profit and related cash-flow forecasts for a reasonable future period, perhaps two years. Although these need not be in the final state required for the proposal, they *must* take account of all the material matters which will affect the future operation of the business, and they *must* be on a prudent basis.

At this stage it will be possible to discuss, preferably with an adviser but possibly with an institution, the approximate purchase price which a financial institution would support, and it may also be possible to obtain on an informal basis reasonably firm indications of interest in proceeding to investment from one or more institutions.

This is, in most cases, the most appropriate time to make an initial, subject to contract, offer. The means by which this initial approach is made varies from case to case, depending very much upon the relationship between the buy-out team and the potential vendor. Most management teams are, however, unaware of how to approach the vendor with an offer, and about the form such an offer should take. Consequently it is quite common for either the adviser or the financial institution to submit an offer on behalf of the management team. This has the advantage that it furthers the initial approach on a professional and arm's-length basis and should also ensure that the subject-to-contract offer is specific and comprehensive.

It is desirable that the negotiations which, it is hoped, will ensue from the initial offer should be conducted either by the professionals or with them attending as advisers. It is unlikely that the team has experience of negotiating company acquisitions and, as has already been intimated, management buy-outs are more difficult to achieve than a straightforward acquisition because of a number of financial and technical constraints. The fundamental point to remember in the negotiations is that the maximum price calculated by reference to the cash flow cannot be exceeded. There is often an inclination on the part of the team to try to clinch the deal even at a price which they know to be too high, but this must be resisted, however difficult it may be to give up when success is apparently within sight.

Pension scheme
One item which will arise in most negotiations, and which can be of such significance as to merit specific mention here, is the pension scheme. Where the buy-out involves the acquisition of a company in which a group pension operates, arrangements will have to be made to set up a separate pension scheme for the bought-out company. Into this scheme should be transferred the appropriate funds from the group scheme to fund the pension entitlements arising from service within the group. The negotiations to agree the transfer value of pension rights are of the greatest importance, since the sums involved can be very large and an inadequate transfer value is likely to have a significant impact on future pension costs. It is also important to commence negotiation on this area as early as possible, because technical aspects can take considerable time to evaluate. In any substantial buy-out it is probably desirable to employ a consulting actuary to assist in the negotiations on this issue.

Tax clearances

Another aspect of the buy-out negotiation which can take time, and consequently needs to be addressed as early as possible, is that of obtaining any necessary tax clearances. Certain transactions in securities can give rise to taxation liabilities through the triggering of anti-avoidance provisions, designed to catch transactions entered into for other than normal commercial reasons. Where it is likely that any aspect of the buy-out might fall within the ambit of such provisions, it is highly desirable to obtain clearance from the Inland Revenue that the particular transactions will not fall foul of them. The Inland Revenue has a statutory maximum of 30 days in which to respond to an application for clearance but if it wishes to raise queries or seek further information, obtaining the clearances can take many weeks. Because of the technical complexity of this area, professional advice needs to be sought as soon as the outline of a possible deal has been reached.

Negotiations with financiers

Throughout this and earlier chapters there has been reference to the desirability of appointing competent professionals to advise on the initial feasibility of the buy-out proposal and on various technical aspects, and to assist in the negotiations with the vendor. Some, but not all, of these functions can also be carried out by the financier. However, it is often overlooked by management teams that they must seek to achieve not just the funding required to enable the buy-out to proceed, but funding on as favourable terms to themselves as is possible. The venture and development capital market is a competitive market, but it is usually little known to those whose business does not regularly impinge upon it. A common and often expensive mistake is to equate a view from a financial institution with professional advice, and to assume that both are dispassionate.

The leading financial institutions operate to high professional standards of technical competence and in general take a responsible attitude to their customers. However, their *raison d'être* is to make money through deals, by backing good management on terms as advantageous to themselves as they can achieve.

The role of the professional adviser, on the other hand, is to look after the interests of his client to the best of his ability, while maintaining high ethical standards. Although the interests of financial institutions, buy-out teams and advisers very often coincide, management should *always* seek impartial financial advice on the terms offered by financiers – except in those rare cases where the management themselves have considerable expertise in the risk-capital markets.

Offers of funding from financial institutions can vary quite significantly. For example, three institutions asked to subscribe £450,000 into a business for which all had received the same proposal variously valued the business at £1.4m., £1.95m. and £2.1m. Thus the respective equity stakes sought by three institutions varied from 32 per cent to 21 per cent. Similarly, on a rather larger buy-out, two leading institutions offering the same level of funding (again from the same proposal) suggested that the management might retain 52 per cent in one case and 60 per cent in the other. Given that all parties agreed that a flotation was likely to be achieved in three years on a capitalised value of, perhaps, £12m., the difference between the two offers as far as the management were concerned could be close to £1m. at flotation.

Similar if less spectacular differences are common in the annual costs of dividends, loan interest and management or directors' fees, and in the particularly sensitive area of the financial institution's initial fees, which can frequently vary between nothing and £50,000 for a medium-sized buy-out. Even with the apparently simple matter of arranging clearing-bank finance, significant savings can be achieved by using professional advice.

Negotiations: the participants

On a more general basis, the complexity of a buy-out for anything but the smallest company is such that achieving it becomes a major management task. Someone needs to keep a finger on the pulse and to ensure that all aspects of the buy-out proceed in as orderly a fashion as possible to completion. It is useful to set out the number of parties who might be involved in a medium-sized buy-out where the consideration passing is perhaps £5m.

1. *Vendor's party*
   Vendor
   Auditor/financial adviser
   Solicitor
   Consulting actuary/pension adviser
   Property consultant

      Tax adviser
      Stockbroker
2.   *Purchaser's party*
      Buy-out team
      Personal financiers (probably bankers) for the team
      Financial adviser/negotiator
      Solicitor
      Consulting actuary/pension adviser
      Property consultant
      Tax adviser
3.   *Financier's party*
      Lead financial institution
      Syndicate financiers
      Solicitors to financing syndicate
      Investigating accountants
4.   *Clearing banker*
5.   *Leasing/finance company*

This list, which is by no means exceptional or exhaustive, illustrates dramatically why co-ordination is necessary. In practice, on very large transactions the lead financiers will normally carry out the co-ordination role; but in the smaller cases the financial adviser or negotiator for the team should probably take this role until, as completion approaches, the solicitors will inevitably need to have close control to ensure that the completion is, in fact, achieved.

Time-scale

As can be seen from the preceding section, a large number of parties and interests are involved in all but the smallest buy-outs. This inevitably places a limit on the speed with which the transaction can be completed. Further delays can occur as a consequence of tax-clearance procedures and the need to issue a Class 4 circular where the vendor is a quoted company (discussed in the following chapter). A significant further source of concern is legal work in relation to properties, where the time taken to obtain appropriate searches can delay the transaction considerably.

Since these and other factors are present to a varying extent in each buy-out it is difficult to be specific about how long it will take to achieve a buy-out. However, as a general guide it is unlikely to be possible to complete such a transaction in less than three months from the team's initial contact with an adviser or financier; for larger transactions four to five months is more realistic. Any major delay in agreeing the terms of the deal with the vendor, or in raising the funding, will increase the time taken.

Conclusions

The negotiations involved in implementing a buy-out are of fundamental importance to the success of the deal. Success is not measured simply by whether the buy-out occurs or not, but crucially concerns achievement of the best terms from both the vendor and the financing institution. It is by no means unknown for management teams to be so keen to purchase their company that they suspend rational judgement. In some cases the result is that they may be unable to realise the full fruits of their labour; in others it may have been preferable not to buy out in the first place.

CHAPTER 7

Some problem areas

Many buy-out transactions are not straightforward. Experience gained since 1980 has enabled negotiators to become familiar with the problems that will need to be dealt with, but even so great care is required in ensuring that the legal rights of creditors, employees, and shareholders in the case of a public listed company, are protected, that liabilities for taxation are minimised and that customers and suppliers remain loyal. These issues are dealt with in this chapter.

Security and financial assistance

In most buy-outs the management contribution is a relatively small proportion of the total purchase price. The balance of the funding is provided, as discussed in Chapters 1 and 4, by financial institutions and banks. To the extent that such finance is supplied as debt, it is likely that some security will have to be provided. Where the management buy-out involves the acquisition of a company, care has to be taken that the transaction does not fall foul of a fairly complex piece of legislation, now contained in sections 151–56 of the Companies Act 1985.

The intellectual rationale behind these much-feared sections was that creditors of a company should be protected from having the net assets of a company which owed them money appropriated or compromised so that other individuals could obtain funds to buy that company.

An illustration helps explain the point. A company formed by a management buy-out team (Newco) agrees to acquire the company in which the team work (Target) for £1m. That sum is to be provided from £150,000 subscribed by the management into Newco, £100,000 ordinary shares and £250,000 preference shares subscribed by a financial institution into Newco, and £500,000 overdraft and term loan secured on the assets of Target.

In this illustration only half (£500,000) of the total amount needed to buy the shares of Target is being provided by the new shareholders in Newco. The balance of £500,000 is being provided from an external source, but the charge being taken over the assets of Target effectively reduces the amount of unencumbered assets in Target available for the benefit of the creditors in general. As an alternative, Target, instead of granting a charge over the assets, could have actually paid £500,000 to Newco to enable it to buy shares in Target. This would have appeared more dramatic, but effectively achieves the same ends.

Section 151 of the Companies Act 1985 prohibits such transactions (referred to as the giving of financial assistance) as a generality. As a consequence of this prohibition, a charge or debenture given to a banker in respect of the £500,000 in the illustration would be invalid and the banker would, in fact, have no security. This explains the extreme nervousness of most bankers faced with a transaction which conceivably might fall within the ambit of s.151. Section 154 of the Companies Act 1985 relaxes the provisions of section 151 in respect of such transactions carried out by a private company.

Even so, there remain some restrictions on these transactions which need very careful consideration. The Act provides that if such financial assistance is to be given, the directors must enquire into the financial circumstances of the company and swear a statutory declaration that, having made such enquiry, they consider that the company will be able to pay its debts as they fall due immediately after the time when financial assistance was given and throughout the 12 months following. This statutory declaration must be supported by a parallel certificate from the company's auditors to the effect that they believe it was reasonable for the directors to have made the declaration. In practice, of course, the auditors will find it necessary to review thoroughly the profits and cash-flow forecasts of the company before giving such a certificate.

Thus although it is now possible for the assets of a bought-out private company to be used to give security for the funds used to buy it, it is vital that the appropriate steps defined by the Act are taken in a thoroughly professional manner. It is likely in any event that the lawyers advising the financiers will wish to be quite satisfied about this point.

Public company buy-outs

The attempted buy-out of a public company exacerbates a number of the inherent difficulties of a private company buy-out. Most importantly this centres on the assertion that managers are employed to work to the best of their ability on their shareholders' behalf and that a willingness to attempt a buy-out suggests that there is a benefit to be had that the managers are prepared to pursue only on their own behalf and not for their paymasters. This of course is present in all buy-outs but is highlighted with a public company because the vendors are presumed not to be professional investors. In practice, since the vast majority of public company shares are held by professional institutional investors the vendors are actually broadly speaking no less capable of making an informed divestment decision than the holding company of a subsidiary for instance.

Other reasons why public company buy-outs are more difficult include the inequality of information available to managers and other potential bidders, market dislike of leverage usually associated with buy-outs and not least the sense that vendors will be passing the opportunity to realise profits to the managers who will sell the shares back to the market when they have done their job. All of these assertions can be refuted. For example, the information available to management is no less than that available to an agreed bidder, the selling shareholder can take cash rather than shares in the leveraged acquisition vehicle, and the reward to managers is achieved only at considerable risk to themselves. Nevertheless, care will need to be taken to rehearse such counter-arguments before the buy-out of a public company is mooted.

Buy-ins

Management buy-ins carry many of the risks of a buy-out but without all the advantages. Principally the buy-in team does not usually have access to the depth and quality of information that would be available to an incumbent management team. Indeed the management buy-in team is in no better position in that respect than any other third-party purchaser and suffers from the disadvantage that it, like a buy-out team, does not have the financial resources to effect the acquisition. As a result both of this dearth of information about the target company's prospects and of the absence of the buy-in team's specific experience of the particular target company the terms on which a buy-in can be financed (reflecting the greater risk being taken) tend to be less favourable than those that would be available to an apparently equally competent buy-out team. Where a buy-in of a public company is attempted, the difficulties raised above in respect of buy-outs of firms listed on a stock market are less likely to arise. However, the incumbent management may resist such a takeover attempt.

Company tax considerations

As far as company taxation matters are concerned, a management buy-out is little different from any other acquisition. The specific technical matters which will need consideration will depend primarily on whether there is a purchase of the issued shares of a limited company or of the assets or undertaking of a company or division.

Acquisition of shares

The usual practice in buy-outs is for the management team to form a new company which acquires the shares in the bought-out company. In this transaction, the parent effectively takes on the past tax history of its new subsidiary when it buys the shares. Although, in a management buy-out, the managers might be expected to know all there is to know about their own company, in practice such knowledge rarely extends to taxation matters because taxation is normally dealt with on a group basis. Consequently it is wise (and probably essential) that they or their advisers should investigate the tax position to determine whether, for example, tax liabilities may arise as a result of technical factors, and at higher rates than anticipated in the profit and cash forecasts.

Where a buy-out company has made losses for tax purposes in the past which are directly available to set against future profits, it is important when negotiating with the vendor to determine its intentions since such losses, subject to certain restrictions, might be available to relieve profits elsewhere in the vendor group. The agreement reached on this point can have a very significant effect on future cash flow, and it is advisable for the team to require certain losses to be available as a condition of their offer.

The availability of tax losses relating to a prior year is subject not only to negotiation with the vendor in respect of group relief but to legislative constraints as well, designed originally to stop the purchase and sale of tax losses. In a straightforward case where the bought-out company is run in very much the same way as prior to the buy-out, losses brought forward will normally be available. However, a number of criteria must be met before this is certain, and professional advice should always be sought in this area.

As is often the case with taxation law, a provision designed to attack an abuse can cause potentially damaging problems. Where the bought-out company owns a property which has been transferred into it from elsewhere in the group at a revalued amount (which is quite a common occurrence), the departure of that company from the group on the buy-out will trigger a corporation tax liability in the company on the notional capital gains computed by reference to the book value of the property at the buy-out and the *original* base value for capital gains tax purposes. While the crystallisation of such a liability may lack either equity or logic, the liability can be real and very material. As a consequence, it is absolutely essential that this particular problem is identified early in the negotiations, because the only way to avoid it is likely to involve revising the structure and probably the terms of the offer.

Acquisition of assets
The basic point to bear in mind here is that a tax benefit to the purchaser will probably produce a tax disadvantage for the vendor, and vice versa. The Inland Revenue will normally review the sale and purchase contracts and follow through the relevant transactions on the tax computation of both vendor and purchaser.

There is, therefore, a basic conflict of interest between vendor and purchaser and these negotiations frequently result in a simple compromise. However, the detailed calculations are complex, and it is unwise for one party to be less well briefed than the other. Again, professional advice will be required.

Stock Exchange requirements for vendor to issue circular

Where the buy-out involves a public listed company, and the buy-out team includes, as it usually does, a director of that company or of a subsidiary, the transaction falls within the ambit of certain regulations of The Stock Exchange. The Stock Exchange 'Yellow Book' describes as 'Class 4' transactions 'those which involve, or involve an associate of, a director, past director, substantial shareholder, or past substantial shareholder of the company (or any other company which is its subsidiary, holding company or a subsidiary of its holding company)'. The Yellow Book requires that the vendor should, before entering into such a contract, notify The Stock Exchange and if applicable clear the transaction with the Panel on Takeovers and Mergers. The Stock Exchange will normally require that a circular is sent to the vendor company's shareholders and that the transaction is ratified at a general meeting of the company, at which the director or directors will be required to abstain from voting. In practice it may be possible to agree with The Stock Exchange that a circular is not required, on the grounds, for example, that the transaction is insignificant in relation to the size of the group. It is, however, important that the vendor discusses the matter with The Stock Exchange before proceeding.

Transitional problems following the buy-out

Most buy-outs result in trading operations which have formerly been carried out by a subsidiary of a large, probably listed, company being carried out in a much smaller and financially weaker entity. The potential implications of this must be anticipated and prepared for before the buy-out occurs. Competitors will, in many cases, seek to use the opportunity which they believe has been afforded by the buy-out to suggest to customers that the bought-out company's viability is now under question and may attempt, by very aggressive pricing, to force the newly bought company out of the market. Customers may respond to either approach by changing suppliers or reducing their requirements.

Suppliers may well be concerned about the creditworthiness of the new business and may arbitrarily and suddenly withdraw credit facilities or restrict the level of supply, at least until they are satisfied with the stability of the company.

Both these problems can have a disastrous effect on cash flow in the early months of trading as an independent company. Management must take this potential threat very seriously indeed in planning the buy-out. The best solution is prevention. Managers should make sure that key customers and suppliers are aware of what is occurring and, in outline at least, of the strength of the financial support for the new vendors. This can be difficult to arrange because, particularly where the vendor is a public company, there may be an embargo on information about the potential buy-out until very shortly before the transaction takes place.

It is also highly desirable to allow a sufficient cushion within the funding arranged for the buy-out to be able to weather a temporary problem. Very highly geared buy-outs with minimal cushion in their total funding are at particularly high risk.

The workforce

A further area of potential problems is the workforce. In many buy-outs, perhaps the better ones, the workforce enthusiastically backs the management's efforts to create an independent company. But both in such cases and in others there is likely to be a legitimate concern about the stability of future employment and the continuation of any group-derived benefits. Again, while the obvious answer is to brief the workforce about what is going on, the embargo referred to earlier may make this difficult and create a climate where inaccurate and disturbing rumours cause a major problem.

After the buy-out it is possible that where a workforce is more concerned with its short-term pay or conditions than its longer-term employment, it may seek to put greater pressure on the company for improvements in pay than prior to the buy-out, on the grounds that the new company is less able to resist. This threat cannot be wholly avoided, which is perhaps why financiers attach great importance to good industrial relations in companies in which they are contemplating investment.

Employee share option plans (ESOPs)

The last few years have seen a very marked increase in the interest in employee share option schemes which, it is believed, will bring greater commitment and better performance in the wake of their implementation. In many of the more substantial buy-outs there is both a willingness on the part of the management team to give options, and a genuine enthusiasm among the workforce to receive them. It is outside the scope of this book to discuss the technical aspects of creating such a scheme, but it is perhaps worth while to look at a problem which is sometimes overlooked.

Implicit in the granting of employee share options is the opportunity, subject to the rules of the scheme, for the employee to realise that investment. However, if the company remains a private company at the time the option falls to be exercised, that share cannot, in practice, be realised unless some form of market can be created. While this may be perfectly possible in a company the size of the National Freight Consortium, it may be less practicable in a much smaller business.

Therefore, before any firm commitment to an employee share option plan is given, it is probably wise to consider all the ways in which employees can be motivated.

Transfer of undertakings and employment protection
The Transfer of Undertakings (Protection of Employment) Regulations 1981 essentially ensure that on the transfer of ownership of a business, all employees working in the business changing hands are automatically deemed to be employed by the purchaser. Thus, employees' contractual rights are protected and the purchaser as the new employer becomes liable for any obligations of the old employer in matters like pay, National Insurance contributions and PAYE. Occupational pension schemes are specifically excluded from the Regulations, though if the purchaser fails to provide a scheme comparable to the one offered by the vendor the employees may have the basis for a claim for compensation on the grounds that they had been constructively dismissed. Sellers are required to take reasonable steps to inform and consult the relevant trade unions about the transfer of ownership and its implications. Failure to do so may involve a complaint by the trade unions to an industrial tribunal.

Where management buying-out do not wish to take on all employees, it is necessary for the vendor to terminate their employment to avoid the purchaser taking on the responsibility. Employees whose contracts are so terminated may be entitled to claim compensation for dismissal unless the vendor can demonstrate that he acted reasonably and that the reasons for dismissal were economic, organisational or technical. The Regulations also cover those who may be indirectly affected by the transfer of ownership, such as head-office staff in the case of a buy-out on divestment.

Where liabilities on the part of the purchaser may arise under these Regulations, the purchaser must take these into account in arriving at the price he should pay to acquire the business.

The contribution of the management team to the value of the business

As noted in Chapters 2 and 5, in some potential buy-out cases much of the value of the business is embodied in the incumbent management team, and it is worth developing the point here. The kinds of businesses involved cover computer software services, specialist financial services, specialist journalist publications, etc. Were management to pay a price for the business based fully on their earnings, they would in effect be buying themselves, and might reasonably be expected to obtain a discount from the vendor. In uncontested buy-outs, such an arrangement might quite readily be forthcoming. Where alternative purchasers are available, the vendor may wish to sell to the highest bidder.

In these circumstances management may have an important bargaining card in the threat of refusal to work for an external purchaser and/or of walking out and setting up in business elsewhere. This walk-out threat may be available in many types of buy-out but is probably most credible where management contribute an important, irreplaceable and specific element of the value of the business. Although such a route may seem attractive, management must be prepared to carry out their threat if their bluff is called. The walk-out option requires extremely meticulous planning by management and their advisers – and not a little nerve! There is a need to ensure that the business can be carried on elsewhere, that finance is available, that management do not breach any contractual restrictions with their employer, that they do not remove any property belonging to the employer or disclose confidential information, and that in preparing to walk out they do not act against their employer's interests. Moreover, should management fail to acquire the business following a walk-out, the prospects for alternative employment must be weighed very carefully. Of course, being made redundant might usefully resolve the contractual obligations which restrict the making of alternative plans. In at least one case where management tried this route and were made redundant by the receiver, they were able to set up in business elsewhere, leaving the receiver with a business he had refused to sell to them and which no one else then wanted to buy. Management did not incur the substantial cost of buying the business, and because the receiver closed the business they were essentially presented with a monopoly position.

This route can be a high-risk strategy, but it does highlight another important point, which is that management ought not to be restricted by tunnel vision into thinking that the standard buy-out route is the only option open to them. It is here that the unbiased help of highly experienced professional advisers can be crucial.

Conclusions

Professional advisers are essential in the successful negotiation of a constantly changing legal and taxation minefield. The importance of dealing successfully with these issues should not be underestimated since failure to do so can jeopardise the completion of the deal and, to the extent that liabilities for taxation might be triggered, incur a needless cash-flow burden on the business.

The need to deal with trading partners and employees is important in ensuring that the buy-out sets off on its independent existence on the right footing, and paves the way for post-buy-out consolidation, future growth and eventual exit. These issues are tackled in the next chapter.

CHAPTER 8

After the buy-out

The excitement generated by the opportunity to acquire the firm in which one is employed and the enthusiasm for the deal to succeed help overcome problems associated with the transfer of ownership. It is not unusual to see the enthusiasm spread itself across all employees of the firm and to manifest itself in increased workforce motivation. When this honeymoon is over a number of serious issues have to be faced, but it is at this point that the management team is perhaps least well prepared to deal with them. The issues involved may be divided into three stages:
- consolidation,
- growth and strategy, and
- exit.

Consolidation

The time of the buy-out and the following months provide an important opportunity to set the newly independent firm in the right direction for future success. The ability of management to effect changes is made easier at this juncture firstly because of the increased freedom of decision taking that acquiring ownership brings and, secondly, because the atmosphere created by the buy-out provides the conditions under which change is more likely to be accepted and assimilated. Striking the right deal, as discussed in previous chapters, is vital and provides an extremely important base on which to consolidate. Financing institutions and advisers may suggest that certain areas of the business require attention to help ensure that finance-servicing obligations are met and that the

company can withstand the pressures of independent existence.
Chapter 3 provided some evidence on post-buy-out profit factors
and cash-flow problems. Consolidation requires attention to the
key business areas of management, employees, trading partners,
product range, cash flow and debtor management, and investment.
A buy-out must show strengths in each of these areas to raise initial
funding, as has been seen earlier, but changes may be necessary to
deal effectively with an independent existence. Of primary concern
is the need to service a substantial debt package. We may consider
each element in turn.

Management
The first tasks of consolidation involve fitting the organisation
structure of the firm to independent existence, getting the right
people into key areas, and making adjustments to the *style* of
management. As may be seen from Table 8.1 the majority of buy-
outs have not required management changes in this consolidation
phase. Companies which had a free managerial rein under the
previous ownership, where for example, family owners took little
direct part in running the business, or where the company was too
peripheral to its parent to attract serious parental control, are likely
to be best placed in this respect.

However, in a significant minority of other cases changes are
required so as to introduce new managers to fill functions
previously either provided by the parent (commonly finance), or
entirely absent. In some cases new management may need to be
introduced where those previously carrying out the function do not
wish to join the buy-out team or are not asked because, for one

Table 8.1 Managerial changes in buy-outs

Sample	Before mid-1983 (%)	Mid-1983–86 (%)
Change in buyout team	9.9	19.1
Divisionalisation	3.6	4.4
Introduction of a new tier of management	11.7	12.6
Removal of a tier of management	9.0	4.4
Recruitment of specialist senior staff	9.0	24.0
Resignation of senior staff	n/a	4.9
Other	11.7	7.1
Sample size	111	182

Note: Percentages sum to more than 100 because of multiple responses.

Source: CMBOR survey of buy-outs between mid-1983 and the first quarter of 1986.

reason or another, they do not fit in. The need to create a new tier of management may arise where a previous owner sought to centralise much of the control to himself, thus losing any benefits to be had from more decentralised decision making. This is perhaps particularly true in family businesses where the founder has been reluctant to let go of what he has created. Subsidiary companies may have been burdened with an organisation structure designed with group needs in mind, but which is inappropriate to its own peculiar market conditions. The time of the buy-out provides the opportunity to recitify the position. In the larger buy-outs, with a diverse product range, divisionalisation may be appropriate to independence, whereas beforehand the product groups were not distinguishable within the parent's own divisionalised structure. It is notable in the later of the two surveys reported in Table 8.1 that there was a greater need to recruit specialist senior staff and to make changes to the buy-out team. The approach adopted by one buy-out, a manufacturer of kitchen furniture, to the development of its organisation structure is of particular interest here. Three major tasks were perceived as necessary in ensuring a successful transition from a subsidiary to an independent structure. First, it was essential to assess the available managerial talent in the company so as to use each individual's capabilities to the full. Second, there was a need to establish a comprehensive information system to allow managerial control to be effective. Third, it was necessary to be able to draw a clear organisation chart which ensured complementarity in skills and effective use of the managerial resources available. The conduct of a management audit by a management consultancy firm was an important element in addressing these tasks. The changes introduced in the organisation structure included a regrouping of functions (so that complementary talents were grouped into five functional areas – Personnel, Finance, Manufacturing, Export, and Marketing). The Finance Department has been strengthened by the inclusion of a Systems section. The Personnel role has been combined with that of company secretary.

Getting the style of management 'right' is also an important element of the consolidation phase, especially in buy-outs of companies requiring a great deal of reorganisation. Requirements for confidentiality have traditionally precluded significant involvement of employees generally at the negotiation phase, but some form of participation can help increase motivation subsequently. This involvement does not generally extend to more strategic issues, but it has proved beneficial at the more tactical and operational levels. The act of buying-out can help management bridge the gulf between hitherto remote owners and employees as a whole. Benefits can be achieved from using employees' knowledge and expertise about the business which had not previously been recognised or proffered. Management buying out have also sought to improve general communication links with employees as a means of fostering cohesion in the workforce. Perhaps the most startling instance of the kinds of benefits which might accrue to the business as a whole in such circumstances comes from the employee buy-out at National Freight Consortium. Following the buy-out, lorry drivers, now with an ownership stake in the business, became a willing source of market intelligence. Prior to the buy-out there had simply been no communication of useful information, picked up in casual conversation with fellow drivers from other firms, to the marketing department.

This additional motivation is frequently encouraged by a revision of existing incentive schemes and the introduction of new ones. Remuneration structures will be changed to give both management and employees additional encouragement to meet the key elements of the buy-out-plan targets such as profits, cash flow and sales. For those who have high levels of personal financial commitments arising from loans taken on to buy shares in the buy-out, remuneration levels may need to be adjusted to allow for this personal debt servicing, although there will be limits on the extent to which this can be achieved.

Employees

Three major employee-related issues are frequently tackled at the time of buy-out, or shortly afterwards, which previously may have been extremely difficult: manning levels, employment contracts, and trade unions recognition.

In total job terms, the earlier survey of 111 buy-outs by Wright and Coyne, showed that 44 per cent of cases had reduced employment at the time of the ownership transfer, with a total fall in full-time employment of some 18 per cent. By the time the survey was carried out, total employment had risen by 11 per cent above its time-of-buy-out level. The survey of 1983 to early 1986 buy-outs conducted by CMBOR showed a much lower level of job loss on buy-out, reflecting the improved economic conditions of this period. As might be expected, buy-outs from receivership accounted for the majority of redundancies. But what the figures show is the benefits from creating a smaller but viable unit, which may subsequently be able to re-employ people. Managers buying-out may obtain two benefits. First, the previous owners can be portrayed as being to blame for the need to make job losses, whilst buy-out managers can portray themselves as the heroes for saving the rest of the jobs. Second, any re-employment can be on a selective basis in terms of taking on only those with skills that are required and who are going to make a full contribution to the company.

Manning levels may be affected by the rationalisation of the management and supervisory structure noted earlier. In particular, a non-working supervisory tier may beneficially be removed in certain cases. Additionally, management may insist on improvements in the flexibility of working practices so as to gain improvements in labour productivity. This issue leads into the wider arena of changes to employee contracts. Buy-outs which involve the complete restart of a business from receivership may be able to benefit most in this respect, though the room to manoeuvre may be limited by the Transfer of Undertakings Regulations 1981. Alternatively, the threat, implied or real, of redundancies arising from trading difficulties may make it easier to negotiate contractual changes with employees. The management team itself may be most likely to be affected through the loss of access to 'top-hat' pension and health benefits that divorce from the former parent may bring – though this may be willingly sacrificed for the potential of capital gains if the buy-out is successful. Certainly the employment contracts of the executive directors and some senior management will be critically examined by the external equity providers to ensure their commitment to the long-term success of the company. Additionally 'Keyman' insurance policies may be taken out on the Chief Executive and other key executives.

It is unusual to find that trade union recognition is removed and where it has occurred, circumstances have been rather special. In one case the restarted company after the buy-out comprised only twelve employees from a previous level of 250, and the management team included two of the former trade union representatives! In another case, employees themselves decided that they did not want the union to be recognised because its officials had been unhelpful in resurrecting the company from receivership. Although trade unions have usually been wary of their members contributing funds to the buy-out, they have not, except in a few cases, openly opposed the buy-out. Management, for their part, have usually been reluctant to remove union recognition if only because it provides a means of communication and a ready-made negotiating structure with the workforce which would otherwise have to be invented. Moreover, there is no suggestion from our examination of buy-outs that they take place only in cases with a demonstrably acquiescent workforce; prior to the transfer of ownership, the level of disputes, of whatever kind, were comparable with that observed for companies generally. As a result of the excitement brought about by the change of ownership and management's attempts to improve communication and decision making, industrial relations post buy-out have generally shown an improvement. In cases where employees have forgone improvements in pay and conditions to aid resurrection of a company it does not mean that they will not seek to make good any loss in the future. The potential for future disputes over this needs to be addressed. Buy-outs on privatisation, particularly from local authorities may be expected to involve more delicate trade union issues. Indeed, there are indications from buy-outs of local-authority bus operations of trade unions being actively involved in buy-out attempts in direct competition with those led by management.

Customers and suppliers

Customers and suppliers of companies bought out in secret are probably totally unaware that a change in ownership has taken place, particularly if trading relationships remain satisfactory. In other cases management can gain a great deal of goodwill from publicising their takeover of the business. Restrictions imposed by impending receivership or tight parental control often place a strain on pre-buy-out trading relationships. Suppliers may face long waits for payment and customers may face delivery delays or difficulties in obtaining the desired product. Less than 10 per cent of buy-outs surveyed by CMBOR lost customers as a direct result of the buy-out, with about 14 per cent losing suppliers. Once these initial losses have been suffered the indication is that trading relationships will be substantially better than pre buy-out. The incentive effect of ownership can frequently prompt management to identify and satisfy customer needs more fully than was previously the case. In buy-outs from receivership, a policy of nurturing key suppliers and customers before the crash is often a crucial element in a successful restart.

Credit management

Credit management is closely linked to customer and supplier relationships. The need to service a highly geared financial package means a corresponding need to maintain a good credit management system. The extent of cash-flow problems if these factors are not dealt with adequately was seen in Table 3.2.

In many cases of divestment buy-outs, wresting control of credit from a parent can be beneficial in itself. For example, a parent company may have a centralised system of credit management, which amongst other things, enables it to use positive cash inflows from one subsidiary to offset negative cash flows elsewhere. The dangers of this policy to an otherwise healthy subsidiary are that it is drained of cash for itself and the credit-payment conditions imposed by the parent may be totally inappropriate to the market-place in which the subsidiary trades. However, whilst independence can enable these problems to be tackled, it also brings others of its own. In the case of receivership buy-outs in particular suppliers may insist on short trade-credit payment periods as they fear another failure. It is clearly important to ensure that the company's initial balance sheet when examined by the supplier's credit analyst gives no cause for concern. In the case of buy-outs which are small, in market-power terms, in relation to their customers and suppliers there is a significant likelihood that they will be squeezed for cash flow by their larger trading partners. Factoring is one way around this problem. The evidence from CMBOR's survey of mid-1983 to early 1986 buy-outs (Table 8.2) shows a high level of reduction in debtor days, increase in creditor days, rationalisation of assets, but little use of factoring.

Table 8.2 Consolidation of financial issues

Financial actions taken post buy-out	Percentage of companies
Debtor days reduced	43.2
Creditor days extended	31.1
Surplus equipment sold	20.8
Surplus land or buildings sold	17.5
Vehicle fleet reduced	13.1
Re-financing of fixed assets	6.0
Factoring of debtors	3.3

Note: Base for % = 182; respondents could take several actions.

Source: CMBOR survey of management buy-outs between mid-1983 and the first quarter of 1986

Product range

A strong market niche is one of the most essential elements in making a buy-out viable, as we have seen in earlier chapters. However, even the most successful products eventually reach the point in their life-cycle when refinement if not replacement is required. The consolidation phase is an appropriate time to deal with those products, identified at the planning stage, which have ceased to make a positive contribution. At the same time new products may also be introduced, free of the restrictions that may have been imposed by a previous owner. However, where a highly geared financial package has to be serviced, a balance in the product range needs to be maintained. Whilst a buy-out can ill afford 'Dog' products, that is those with poor prospects, it also has to be wary of potential 'Stars' which although having substantial growth potential, place high demands on cash, at least in the short term. We have more to say about these issues in the section on growth and strategy. It should be emphasised, however, that if poor products are only *identified* at the consolidation stage the bought-out company may be faced with a major problem. Such difficulties may arise if unexpected downturns in the markets for the products occur, perhaps due to deteriorating macro-economic conditions or the introduction of a revolutionary new product by a competitor. This emphasises the need to conduct the planning stage with a high degree of thoroughness. The survey of mid-1983 to early 1986 buy-outs conducted by CMBOR showed that 62.3 per cent of respondents introduced new products after the transfer of ownership which they would not otherwise have done (Table 8.3). For the most part these involved refinements and replacement of products in existing markets. However, there was a significant incidence of the extension of product diversity. There was little evidence of a desire to withdraw completely from a market, but a notable degree of rationalisation of product ranges. These changes indicate a much more dynamic pattern of product behaviour than might have been expected given the traditional view of the kind of companies suitable for a buy-out. However, the UK buy-out market has always been one where growth of companies has been sought, perhaps because of the key roles played by venture-capital firms. Even the large debt-financed buy-outs currently seen in the UK have tended to require product development. As a result, the need for investment expenditure requires careful attention.

Table 8.3 Post-buy-out product development

Percentage of companies introducing new products which they would not otherwise have done	62.3
	% of companies
Refinements of existing products	6.0
New products in same market area	19.1
New products to move into new market	6.6
Refinements of existing products and new products in same market areas	8.7
Refinements of existing products and new products to move into new market	0.5
Refinement of existing products and new products in both existing and new markets	11.5
New products for both existing and new markets	9.3
Percentage of companies ceasing production of products as a result of the buy-out	16.9
	% of companies
Replacement by new version	0.5
Desire to withdraw from market	3.8
Rationalisation of product range	9.8
Other	3.1

Source: CMBOR survey of management buy-outs between mid-1983 and the first quarter of 1986.

Investment

As with 'Stars', investment places demands on funds at a time when a bought-out company is perhaps least well placed to service them. Ideally, either a buy-out will have few investment needs in the medium term, or the finance package arranged at the time of the change in ownership can make allowances for essential investments. There may be a particular need to replace certain machinery and equipment where the firm has been starved of investment funds prior to buy-out. Buy-outs of a company which is much reduced after receivership may require smaller premises. In some of the larger buy-outs, the consolidation phases may involve the divestment, disposal or closure of certain sub-elements for both profit and cash-flow reasons as well as cases where the divesting parent insists that management take all or nothing so as not to be left with further reorganisation costs. A similar position may arise in cases of buy-outs from receivership. If the price agreed by management has been well negotiated, consolidation may enable useful cash contributions to be realised. The CMBOR survey found that 43.7 per cent of buy-outs purchased equipment and plant which they otherwise would not have done, with about 25 per cent purchasing vehicles and land and buildings. Asset rationalisations were noted earlier. Asset disposals as part of the buy-out deal are still unusual in the UK compared to the US, although there have been one or two recent large exceptions. Interestingly, MFI-Hygena planned to dispose of certain stores in order to reduce indebtedness after it failed to meet its original flotation target date.

Growth and strategy

Some buy-outs do not make it beyond the consolidation stage, 3i for example, estimate a failure rate amongst buy-outs of about one in ten. Others which do not fail absolutely, nevertheless show little growth, if any. The Wright and Coyne study of 111 pre-1983 buy-outs showed that amongst those which were greater than two years old, about 50 per cent recorded either substantial or slight stable growth in profits and sales. In about 30 per cent of cases fluctuating fortunes were in evidence, whilst for the rest sales and profits declined. Amongst buy-outs less than two years old about 50 per cent had performed better than expected, with a little under 40 per cent showing profits greater than expected. The more recent CMBOR survey found that over 60 per cent of firms improved trading profits and sales compared with pre buy-out. Moreover, 50 per cent claimed to have performed better than their business plan in terms of profits. But almost 33 per cent were performing worse than their business plan and 17 per cent were doing less well than before the buy-out. Numerous factors are at work here which influence performance in either a positive or negative way. Most notable in this respect are industrial and market factors. As productivity gains and the benefits from the removal of parental overheads tend to be one-off advantages at the time of the buy-out, there is a subsequent need to plan and carry out a strategy for growth based on success in the market-place. It is necessary to maintain a highly motivated and capable management team who will reach the correct decisions about which markets to occupy and how to get there. We shall first of all discuss the elements of a buy-out's corporate strategy and then address the issues which involve management's role in developing such a strategy.

Corporate strategy

There are, of course, general principles of corporate strategy which apply to all firms, whether or not they are management buy-outs. Although this is not a book about strategy it is useful to outline the main elements and then see how they apply in the case of buy-outs.

The essential elements of a general corporate strategy are shown in Figure 8.1. The starting point in the development of corporate strategy is a comparison of the performance of the set of activities currently engaged in with the business objectives. Performance-Gap Analysis essentially involves the projection over the foreseeable future of the firm's current performance trends, assuming no major shift of policy occurs. This projection is compared with what would be required over the same period for the firm's objectives to be achieved. The gap between the two projections provides the starting point for identifying causes and solutions. An initial solution may, of course, be to revise the company's objectives to a more realistic level. In developing policy options, a firm will engage in strategic search. Strategic search involves both an examination of the external competitive environment in which the firm operates, or is considering entering, and an analysis of the internal processes by which the firm adds value to incoming basic materials.

Clearly these external and internal aspects are closely inter-related. The efficiency with which a firm carries out its activities is directly related to the effectiveness with which it deals with its environment. A fit is required between what is required in the market-place and what the internal activities of the business can provide. Competitive strategies provide the general approach to be adopted in dealing with the market environment so as to achieve the firm's objectives. Strategies should build upon the relative strengths of the firm in relation to the market that it serves. Possible strategies may place emphasis on one of the following. A firm able to reap the benefits of economies of large scale may seek to pursue a strategy of being the low-cost producer in the market. Alternatively, a firm may aim to pursue a strategy whereby it occupies a strong market niche with few if any competitors, i.e., it differentiates itself from its competitors in terms of such things as product, marketing approach, etc. A third option is to pursue a focus strategy whereby the firm directs attention to serving *one segment* of the market to the exclusion of others and does it either in terms of exploiting a cost advantage or by differentiating itself from competitors and so serves the needs of consumers that are not met by other producers. Importantly, a firm or a division within a firm ought not to attempt to pursue a mixture of these three strategies. As shown in Figure 8.1, action taken to pursue these strategies can involve a variety of approaches. Growth may be achieved by either internal expansion and/or acquisition activity and involve diversification into related or unrelated product areas. Integration may be

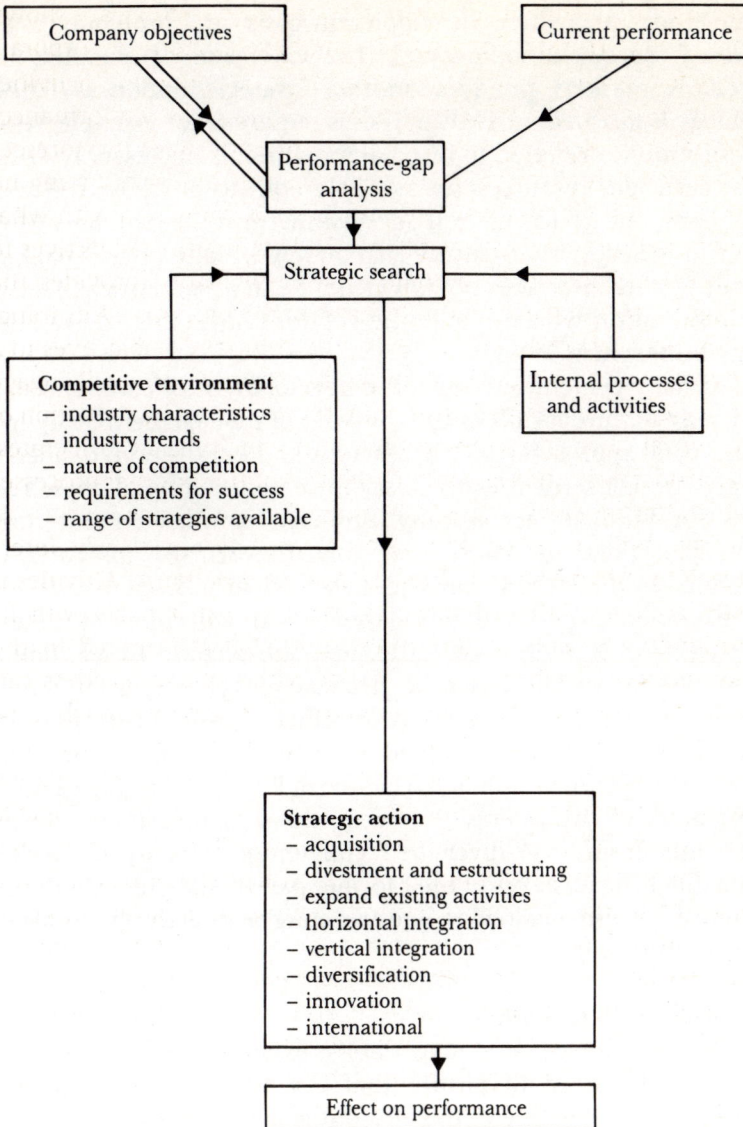

Figure 8.1   Elements of a corporate strategy

pursued as a means of gaining the benefits of producing more than one product. Where this involves the various products in several stages of production, vertical integration is achieved, where a related range of final products are produced, horizontal integration obtains. A firm may choose to pursue a leader role in new product innovation or, where development costs are prohibitive, gain through successful innovation. The extension of expertise into overseas markets provides another strategic option. Whatever strategy is pursued, careful analysis is required. For example, where acquisition is preferred to internal growth, it is necessary to ensure that sufficient resources are available both to purchase the target company and to integrate it successfully into the acquirer. Moreover, it is necessary to ensure that an appropriate price is paid and that the purchaser does not fall victim to an asymmetric possession of information whereby only the vendor knows the true worth of the business he is selling.

For management buy-outs, the development of corporate strategy may require a shift in the thinking of management away from the type of approach which characterised the transition to independence. In one sense it is necessary to cease thinking of oneself as a buy-out, and to act as any ordinary commercial enterprise. However, there are both limitations to such an approach and benefits from drawing on the lessons learnt from buying-out. Management experience during the buy-out will colour attitudes to strategy and is addressed in the next sub-section. In addition, at least in the early phases of strategic development, it will be necessary to bear in mind the constraints imposed by the nature of the financial package adopted on buy-out. Where substantial finance-servicing costs have to be met, a limit may be placed on the company's ability to engage in acquisition or investment activity. Buy-outs from over-diversified conglomerates may do well to remember the mistakes of their former parent and pursue a strategy where expertise obtained in one area may be directly applicable in a new product area.

Management and strategy

Essentially two sets of managerial issues present themselves. First, there is the need to ensure that the unusually high level of motivation at the time of the buy-out is maintained. Second, there is a need for management to redirect their style of thinking to more strategic issues rather than shorter-term ones.

The high level of motivation arising from the excitement of becoming the owner of the business for which one has previously been an employee can easily be dissipated when the transition is successfully completed and attention once more focuses upon the more routine matter of the day-to-day running of the business. This point may be particularly true where the markets in which the buy-out operates are rather stable and show little growth. It can be an even worse problem where management do not feel themselves to be the recipients of any substantial monetary rewards for their efforts over the preceding two or three years. This point raises the question of exit by the team. Although exit is an issue which must be addressed in the planning and negotiation stages of the buy-out it is expositionally convenient to deal with it in detail below.

The problem of maintaining motivation also extends to managers and other employees outside the core team, as they too may have been drawn up into the euphoria of the buy-out. In the early recession-led buy-outs from receivership, employees generally may have needed to be reminded of the stark alternative to the current situation, but, as with the management team, loss of motivation may be derived from a desire to catch up the 'sacrifices' made when the buy-out was launched. In buy-outs in general, particularly in the more successful ones, problems may be experienced where employees as a whole observe what they consider to be inequitable returns being earned by the buy-out team, even though in fact such returns may be justifiable rewards from risk taking. In those buy-outs which have obtained a USM or full stock-market listing, employees as a whole do have the opportunity to obtain an equity stake (but not on the terms that the buy-out team obtained originally). In the case of Metsec, for example, 60 per cent of employees purchased shares at the time of the USM quote in October 1985. The existence of share option schemes may encourage those entitled to them to take them up and effect an exit so as to realise their capital gain. The extension of employee share-option schemes to a wider circle of employees, now that legislative changes have made it a more attractive practical policy, may be a useful longer-term means of improving motivation and retaining key employees. A number of buy-out teams have indicated that they would have liked to extend share ownership at the time of buy-out but were precluded from doing so because of the need for secrecy in negotiations. It is not clear to what extent they have tried to remedy this problem subsequently. The development of Employee Share Ownership Trusts may make it easier to introduce general employee share ownership at the time of buy-out.

Where a buy-out does display marked growth, the team's motivation may be maintained as it continues to see rewards for its efforts. However, rapid growth does pose another delicate problem – that of the capability of the team. Some team members may be excellent line managers, able to co-ordinate production effectively, to maintain a dynamic and effective sales force, or to keep a tight control of budgets. Others may be very good at building up new product divisions in an entrepreneurial fashion. However, success in these areas does not necessarily mean that such managers can and will develop into good strategic thinkers. It is a problem which is evident throughout organisations generally. In buy-outs the difficulty comes when the realisation that some members of the original team are not capable of dealing with the new demands required of them has to be faced. Since an essential element of setting up a buy-out in the first place is often continuity of management, retirement may not offer a way out. In the Wright and Coyne study of 111 buy-outs completed before mid-1983, for example, only 16 per cent of team members covering the Managing Director, Sales and Production functions were over 55 years of age and only 7 per cent of team members covering finance were in this age bracket.

It may take a great deal of courage for a team member to accept that someone else should be carrying out his or her strategic tasks. For the success of the company there is little room for sentiment. If such prospects were to be effectively blocked, able people may leave. There is, therefore a need to adopt a positive view of team enhancement. Original team members may still be seen to have important tactical and operational roles to play even where new members need to be brought in to tackle the more strategic issues. Where new members are introduced, the question of their equity stake in the business needs to be addressed. The approach adopted is really a matter for negotiation. On the one hand, an equity stake may be seen to provide an important incentive to new members of the team, in the same way as original members themselves benefited from such effects. On the other hand, original team members may be reluctant to 'give-away' some of what they have worked hard at and taken risks in making successful. Enhanced salary and profit-sharing is one means of giving new members an attractive incentive package.

Alternatively, it may be argued that giving new members an equity stake may have the effect of significantly increasing performance of the company, so that original members benefit from having a smaller percentage of a much larger cake but an absolute gain. Where flotation occurs, spreading the incentive effect of equity stakes is in any case more easily achieved.

Exit

Sooner or later both the financier and the management team in a buy-out are looking for a means of realising some or all of their investment in the company. Given the now mature state of development of the buy-out market-place, many buy-outs have already had to deal with this issue, but many more still have to address it. Exit may be sought by either party for reasons of both success and failure and may be partial or complete. The exit process can be an important period of transition which needs to be handled as carefully as the initial act of buying-out. The method and timing of exit may highlight conflicting objectives between institutions and buy-out teams. One method of dealing with this problem, particularly in larger deals, is to use a ratchet mechanism, as noted in Chapter 5. Ratchets enable management's equity stake to vary depending upon the buy-out's performance, which may include market capitalisation on flotation or trade sale by a certain date. Hence management may have a very strong incentive to develop the company as their wealth depends upon meeting certain well-defined targets. In the survey conducted by CMBOR of buy-outs completed between mid-1983 and early 1986, a little under 25 per cent of cases had financial structures with management's equity dependent upon a ratchet. Successful operation of the ratchet could result in management switching from a minority stake to having more than 50 per cent of the equity in 33 per cent of cases. In almost 66 per cent of cases the ratchet was related to performance targets, usually specific targets for each year or cumulative profits over a period. The remaining 33 per cent of ratchets related to exits and other targets including redemption of preference shares on realisation. Management's incentive to seek a timely flotation or trade sale may be increased by ratchet conditions which vary over time. Hence, the longer realisation is delayed the more management may have to perform at high levels over a longer period in order to achieve the same target equity percentage. Moreover, participating dividends or heavy debt repayment schedules may cut in beyond a certain date, providing an extra motivation to seek a realisation. Ratchet mechanisms are contentious as seen in Chapter 5 since they are not applicable in all cases (e.g., smaller buy-outs with predictable profit returns) and can cause disputes between management and institutions (e.g., over the interpretation of targets), can produce inappropriate action by management (e.g., seeking short-term returns at the expense of the long-term), and can lead to institutions receiving high short-term returns and lower medium-term ones (e.g., where exit occurs sooner than anticipated and the gains from gearing are diluted).

Exit routes

The two most obvious exit routes are flotation on a stock market and sale to a third party.

The main goal for a large proportion of buy-outs is probably to obtain flotation either on The Stock Exchange proper or the Unlisted Securities Market (USM). A few have floated on the Third Market, now merged with the USM. Initially the USM provided the more likely exit route in buy-outs, mainly because its entry requirements are less stringent than for a full listing. Many of those buy-outs which obtained a USM quote did so with the hope of achieving a full listing in the fullness of time.

The USM was introduced in November 1980 as a means of overcoming the restrictive conditions for obtaining a full listing. The two main conditions for a USM quotation are:
- usually a satisfactory two year trading record;
- a minimum of 10 per cent of shares to be made available to the public.

There is no obligation to present an accountants' report provided that no marketing of securities is taking place (the 'Introduction' route). Table 8.4 provides a detailed comparison of the differences between the USM and a full listing.

Table 8.4 Differences between the markets

	Official List	USM
Trading record	3 years	2 years (property co. 3 years)
Advertisement in national newspapers (a) introduction	1 small box	1 small box
(b) placing	1 small box (marketing below £2m or above £2m joint with another broker) or 1 full prospectus above £2m and direct to the public)	1 small box
(c) offer for sale	2 full prospectuses (if capitalisation of company less than £15m, requirement as for a placing)	1 small box (more in practice)

Table 8.4 continued

Entry fee	£120 to £81,780	50% of Official List scale charge
Annual fees	£1,200 to £21,140	£1,780 or 50% of Official List scale charge if nominal equity value £10m or more
Annual levy	£350	£125
Minimum equity to be held by outside shareholders	25%	10%
Minimum market capitalisation	£700,000 (although in practice this is likely to be too small)	No lower limit
Accountants' short-form report for prospectus	Required: 3 years	Required: 5 years (to be reduced to 3 years). May not be required for an 'introduction'
Adequacy of working capital	Directors' declaration and sponsor's comfort letter required (in practice most sponsors will require an accountants' report on this)	Directors' declaration required but sponsors are not obliged to provide a comfort letter to The Stock Exchange (in practice most sponsors will require an accountants' report on this)
Agreement to be signed	Applicants accept the continuing obligations set out in Admission of Securities to Listing (the 'Yellow Book') by virtue of their application for and subsequent maintenance of listing	General Undertaking
Circular to shareholders required if acquisition represents:	15% or more of existing assets/profits. Accountants' report required if 25% or more. Listing particulars required if 10% or more of equity or any debt securities to be issued as consideration	35% or more of existing assets/profits. Accountants' report required.
Major transactions	Shareholders' approval required if acquisition or disposal represents 25% or more of existing assets/ profits	Shareholders' approval required if acquisition or disposal represents 75% or more of existing assets/ profits.

As management buy-outs are usually companies of several years' standing, albeit in a different guise, the three-year trading record requirement may frequently be circumvented although a potential problem arises for those buy-outs which are asset purchases.

Table 8.5 provides evidence from a Spicer & Oppenheim survey of the advantages and disadvantages of obtaining a public quotation for smaller companies.

Two factors stand out very clearly as the main advantages of coming to a stock market; the ability to raise further money and status and prestige. The strength of views about raising further finance is particularly interesting given the state of markets in smaller companies' shares following the events of October 1987. Other factors rate much less in importance than found in earlier studies of companies' attitudes to flotation.

For many buy-outs, flotation may provide an important juncture at which to introduce employee share option schemes or merely an opportunity for employees to purchase shares, which may not have been feasible at the time of the buy-out. However, a growing number of buy-outs appear to be introducing at least the mechanism for employee share option schemes at the time of buy-out. Shop-floor meetings with groups of employees are frequently used as an important device for promoting the attractiveness of employee share participation in much the same way as they are likely to have been used to explain initially the implications of the buy-out.

Through the benefit of making it easier to raise further money, flotation may also provide the opportunity to pursue a growth

Table 8.5 Benefits and disadvantages of a public quotation

Benefits	%	Disadvantages	%
Easier to raise further money	64	More in the public eye	39
Status and prestige	59	Legal requirements to be met	22
Introduction of employee share option scheme	15	Six-monthly financial reporting	17
Improved morale of employees	12	Stock Exchange obligations	17
Ability to make acquisitions	11	Constraints on directors' freedom of action	15
Marketability of shares	10	Some loss of control	13
Closer contact with professional advisers	8	Need to improve performance	13
Recognition of company name	7	Public accountability	5

Note: Percentages do not total to 100 because of multiple responses.

Source: 'Going Public, Benefit or Burden – a survey of smaller quoted UK companies', conducted by City Research Associates on behalf of Spicer & Oppenheim, April 1988.

strategy through acquisition. A quoted company can issue shares to pay for acquisitions, depending upon the state of the stock market, whereas a private company is usually restricted to the use of internally generated or borrowed cash. However, the evidence from the survey indicates that the ability to make acquisitions is an important benefit to only a few firms.

Table 8.5 also indicates the disadvantages of a flotation, though it is noticeable that feelings are less strong in this respect than about the benefits. The main concern is over publicity. Publicity may be attractive when everything in the company is progressing well, but such may not be true in more difficult times and is very often outside the company's control. Stock analysts may be felt to be over-zealous in their pursuit of information on the company while being in the public eye also increases the pressure to perform with emphasis on the short term. Requirements to pay a continuing and preferably increasing dividend stream may pose cash-constraint problems in managing the business although such pressures have been present in many buy-outs since the purchase took place.

The costs of flotation can be as much as 10 per cent of the sums raised, particularly where smaller amounts are involved. The comparative costs of raising a given sum on the USM or via a full listing are affected by the more stringent requirements for the latter, particularly advertising. However, USM entry costs have risen sharply in recent years, narrowing the cost differential with the main market. Crucial elements in any flotation are to ensure that it goes smoothly without disrupting unduly the normal operating activity of the business, and to time it correctly so as to fit in with the business-growth strategy and optimise the amount of new funds raised. This last point involves setting the flotation price correctly, which itself requires not only analysis of general and sectoral market trends but also how brokers are likely to view the strengths and weaknesses of the individual company. It is in these areas that the continuing relationship with the adviser, built up since the buy-out, can be essential for success.

Some dilution of control may be expected on flotation, but given the fairly low percentage of shares which have to be made available, this may well be outweighed by the benefits of realising some personal capital gains and raising extra funds for the company which will usually enable the preference shares to be redeemed and bank borrowings to be reduced. In any case, the market will expect the continuing commitment of the team which has built up the company to maintain the track record and the share-placing agreement may effectively prevent management from selling further shares over the next year. Should management envisage realising a very large proportion or even all of their investment then an outright sale is probably a preferred exit route.

Perhaps the most important aspect of a flotation is that it enables financiers at least in principle to realise some or all of their investment in the business, and put a value on the remainder. Where the original deal was a syndicated one, flotation enables changes in the relative positions of the members of the consortium to be achieved. In a few cases where the buy-out looks well set for substantial further growth some syndicate members have increased their shareholdings. Changing the relative positions of consortium members may also enable important changes in the nature of the capital structure to be effected.

CMBOR has identified 174 stock-market flotations (Table 8.6), of buy-outs with a majority floated on the USM. However, in 1987 and 1988, the relative importance of the USM declined with full market flotations comfortably exceeding those on the second market. Part of the reason for this shift relates to the increasing size of buy-outs coming to market, making the USM less appropriate. Additionally, as noted already, cost differentials between the two markets have narrowed. The total number of flotations fell from the 1986 peak in 1987 and 1988, a direct result of the events of October 1987. As well as liquidity on the USM appearing to have been adversely affected to a greater degree than for the official market, the adverse stock-market conditions in late 1987 and early 1988 also resulted in a lengthening of the average time taken for

Table 8.6 Flotations of management buy-outs

	Official list	USM	Third market	Total
1980	0	1	–	1
1981	2	2	–	4
1982	1	4	–	5
1983	2	7	–	9
1984	6	6	–	12
1985	6	22	–	28
1986	15	21	–	36
1987	21	9	4	34
1988	21	13	0	34
1989 (end June)	3	5	1	9

Note: This table excludes stocks quoted on OTC markets
or the Granville ICE. Markets shown are the original
markets on which companies were floated and exclude
transfers from one market to another.

Sources: Stock Exchange and CMBOR.

buy-outs to float. In 1986 the average time taken to float was 4 years 1 month, falling to 3 years 7 months in 1987 and rising again to 4 years 1 month in 1988. However, the recovery in stock-market conditions in the latter half of 1988 and into 1989 has meant that periods to float have begun to shorten once more. Price/Earnings ratios at flotation, though, remain below their peak levels of 15.6 seen in 1987. For 1988, the average P/E ratio of buy-outs coming to market stood at 11.3.

Despite the stock-market recovery in 1989, illiquid markets for the less well-known stocks contributed to dissatisfaction with this form of exit route. Indeed, in the first half of 1989 only nine buy-outs were floated as against 25 in the corresponding period of 1988.

Sale to a third party is increasingly seen as an attractive alternative to flotation. In the years 1985–88, 134 trade sales of buy-outs have been identified, with this realisation route comfortably exceeding flotations after 1987 (Table 8.7). For smaller buy-outs or those without the requisite track record for obtaining a stock-market quotation, trade sale may be the most feasible exit option. Companies which pursued the asset-purchase route to buy-out may be particularly affected in this way. However, the issues involved go beyond this particular problem.

For institutional investors, a trade sale in the post-October 1987 climate may have its attractions. Sale may be effected for most industrial sectors at a premium over the likely stock-market flotation price and the problems of selling below alpha stocks in markets that remain thin and with wide spreads, can be avoided. Many managements may be unwilling to accept a trade bid because of the loss of independence it would entail and the consequences for future development of the business. But this argument may not always be applicable and it may be useful for all parties to consider at an early stage that trade sale may have important attractions.

In some buy-outs sale to an outside party may be the only way to remove an onerous debt burden which was taken on in the

Table 8.7 Trade sales from UK buy-outs

	1985	1986	1987	1988	1989Q2
Sale of unquoted MBO to another company	12	33	38	48	30
Sale of quoted MBO to another company	0	11	10	20*	4
Total	12	44	48	68	34

* Includes 3 mergers and 4 buy-ins

Source: CMBOR.

expectation of a rate of growth which in the event did not materialise. The failure to meet such a schedule could limit reinvestment and long-term growth as well as personal salary enhancement. Pressure may come from financiers who are disappointed at the rate of progress and wish to get out of a venture whilst they can.

Trade sale may be attractive where management are not really strong enough to lead a floated company or where splits in the buy-out team make flotation extremely difficult (see below). It may also need to be recognised that for some companies quoted plc status may not be especially glamorous. Thinly traded markets may make it difficult to issue paper to make acquisitions. A close positive relationship with institutional investors may be replaced by a more intrusive one with analysts who may have very different interests. Dilution of equity holdings may make a company vulnerable to a hostile take-over bid.

For the longer-term success of the business, there may be very good reasons for seeking a friendly take-over. The initial niche market strength of many buy-outs may become a longer-term weakness. The recent growth of take-over activity generally in the UK, in which context buy-outs have to be placed, has seen a great deal of emphasis placed on the achievement of leading market positions. Buy-outs, even successful ones, may find themselves no longer of a size and financial strength to remain independent. A white knight acquisition may give access to new markets and distribution outlets which could not otherwise be achieved.

Sale to an outside party may be attractive where management are no longer concerned about independent control and wish to take their gains, or where they see better career enhancement prospects within a larger organisation – possibly a reversal of their original reasons for wanting to buy-out. Alternatively, of course, outright sale may be at a price which is too attractive to refuse, enabling managers to leave the company and pursue other objectives, such as, for example, buy-in opportunities.

Outright sale raises important issues for both the purchaser and the vendor. If, as is usually the case, the core management team are an essential element in the viability of a buy-out, the prospective purchaser needs to be sure either that some of the team will continue to play an important role, at least in the transition phase, or that capable second-line management can be promoted to replace them, or that there are sufficient resources in the parent to take on the task. Integrating a new acquisition is a perennially difficult problem which should not be underestimated. One of the major impediments to successful integration is where the corporate cultures of the parent and the acquiree are fundamentally incompatible. Where an acquisition involves a buy-out which has enjoyed a significant degree of independence and where the concept of the buy-out has generated significant motivational effects, integration needs to be well thought-out and handled with care. Where management do remain with the company after the sale, their motivation may be maintained through service contracts and significant equity stakes in the new parent.

For the vendors it is essential to plan what is to be done with the proceeds of sale. These intentions may themselves have a direct impact on the nature of the sale. Taxation implications are the obvious factor to be taken into account, but whether it is better to receive payment in cash or shares and issues about continuing involvement in some capacity also need to be thought through. In general, sale of the buy-out will have major personal taxation implications.

Some buy-outs, clearly, do have significant growth potential to be realised as independent companies at the time of flotation. Trade sale may become the optimum strategy at a later date. Moreover, flotation may be a means by which the availability of a company can be more transparent and a subsequently higher exit premium realised. In 1986–88, 41 sales of quoted buy-outs to other companies have been identified (Table 8.7).

Several hundred smaller buy-outs may now be faced with the problem of how to realise the investment of financiers and management. Aggressive participating dividends may put pressure on management to restructure or seek an exit. Those buy-outs which are small in relation to competitors and with a still relatively highly geared balance sheet may find difficulty in establishing financial credibility with large potential customers as well as trade creditors. Hence smaller companies may be trapped in a vicious circle which prevents them from expanding their customer base or obtaining a healthier balance sheet. Trade sale may provide a means of achieving financial stability and background strength.

A third exit route is provided by receivership, which has occurred in some cases, though the failure rate in buy-outs is considerably less than for new start-ups. Some buy-out deals may have been made on the basis of over-optimistic expectations or where a sudden unforeseen downturn in the market places the company in jeopardy. Restructuring the financial package may enable the debt repayment burden to be eased, whilst further rationalisation may help survival prospects. Where there is serious under-performance but not yet receivership, institutions are likely to require a major restructuring of finance and the company, including enforced changes in the management team possibly by means of a buy-in.

Purchase of the company's own shares also provides a possible exit route. The Companies Act 1981 enabled, for the first time in the UK, the use of a company's funds to buy its own shares back from shareholders. Such a move is possible in a company with a strong positive cash flow and can be attractive to financiers and management. Financiers can effect an exit whilst receiving a premium on their initial investment. Management do not have the problem of diluting their interests in the company which sale to others may produce and indeed will enhance their ownership stake and maintain long-term control. Moreover, management are not faced with the problem of having to raise the money to buy back shares from personal resources, which would have been necessary under the previous legislation. There are difficult taxation issues with this exit route. It may only be tax effective where it can be demonstrated that the transaction is for the benefit of the business. In addition, this option may be more appropriate for buy-outs where institutions have a minority shareholding. It can produce acute valuation problems and if not considered in the context of an overall package may leave the firm with an inappropriate capital structure.

Existing institutions wishing to maintain a longer-term relationship may inject additional funds to finance growth. However, this can be a complex operation in large deals with many syndicate partners and equity ratchets that require renegotiation. Management may also be concerned at the possibility of continued over-close control by institutions. Capital restructurings enable management and institutional equity investors to realise some or all of their investment by means of an extension of senior debt and the possible introduction of mezzanine funds. This route provides a clear exit route for larger buy-outs wishing to remain independent during a period of relatively weak stock market trading. Continuity is provided by the senior debt lenders and a reduced institutional equity element.

Occasionally, a new set of investors may replace the original institutions whilst the company remains private. Through this route, incumbent management may be able to increase their equity stake, possibly with a new set of incentives. Mezzanine debt may be appropriate in refinancing those firms for whom high levels of good-will and institutional equity stakes make it difficult to raise sufficient secured debt or effect share buy-backs. A second buy-out may effectively take place with new institutional shareholders, amendments to Articles of Association and institutional rights, the establishment of another newco and extension of share-ownership to a wider group of employees. A second buy-out may also occur where a new incumbent team take over on the retirement of the original buy-out members. A buy-in may also be a possibility in these circumstances.

Clearly, flotation and trade sale are not the only alternatives which may enable institutions to achieve their target rate of return and meet management's objectives. The above alternatives which allow at least partial realisation by investors but ensure the continuing independence of the business are likely to come into increasing focus. The growing size of the UK buy-outs and the different requirements of syndicate members in the larger trans-actions can be expected to result in the growth of markets which allow partial realisation.

The form that these alternative realisation routes will take will vary significantly depending on specific factors relating to each individual buy-out. The main influences are likely to be: size, initial purchase price, post-buy-out performance, prospects, participating dividends, gearing, management's objectives and the diversity of investors.

Exit and the team

Throughout the discussion of buy-outs, emphasis has been placed on the importance of the cohesion of the management team. The exit issue may either reinforce or place strains upon the team. At one level partial exit effected via a Stock Exchange listing signals a degree of success achieved by the team. Such success can provide the basis for future expansion so as to remain a strong independent company. Where team members are not within sight of retirement age and consider that the growth of the company provides the best route for their career development, the cohesion of the team is enhanced. Moreover, a member may be reluctant to leave for fear of letting down his colleagues. It is important, therefore, that the opportunities and resources for expansion are available to the bought-out company and that an important motivating factor for management is the desire to exercise control over their own company. The spirit of and opportunities for entrepreneurship must remain. In a sufficiently large team with a good support group of management, replacement of members who wish to retire can be effected quite smoothly, particularly where a stock-market listing is available.

For some buy-outs, however, the exit issue can be more problematical for the team. Consider a fairly small team of three members, in a buy-out with modest growth which has turned itself from being an unwanted, insignificant and under-funded subsidiary of a large company into a viable entity. Let us say that the sales director is, some three years after buy-out, within five years of retirement but that the other two members of the team are in their early forties. Such a case is not unusual in many buy-outs. The three members of the team have for the past three years subjugated their individual interests in order to establish the buy-out. Given the company's modest growth from a small base it is still some way from obtaining a USM quote. However, the objectives of each individual member begin to surface. The production director, having successfully dealt with the technical issues in this company now requires a challenge and is thinking of starting a new company.

The managing director is also looking for a new challenge either in terms of acquiring another company which requires turnround or through enhanced career prospects that acquisition by a larger company might offer. The sales director, beginning to think of retirement, is becoming increasingly unwilling to consider risky ventures which might jeopardise his realisable share of the company. It also needs to be borne in mind that modest growth limits the career prospects of second-line management with a consequent adverse effect on staff turnover rates. The management team is therefore in a dilemma. Resolution of the problem may require careful planning with the help of the business's financial adviser if it is to be achieved to the satisfaction of all concerned. It is important to accept early on that such problems can arise and act accordingly. Otherwise, irreconcilable differences between members of the team may end in a solution that nobody wants and that essentially destroys the fruits of years of hard work and commitment.

Conclusions

Three important post-buy-out stages have been identified. The first concerns consolidation of the various elements of the business so as to set it on course for a successful independent existence. Such activity is about the filling of key gaps in the organisation where functions were perhaps previously carried out by the former parent, achieving an appropriate level of employees, improving trading relationships, fine-tuning internal control systems, etc. The second element of post-buy-out development relates to preparation for growth and the development of a longer-term strategy. To some extent the buy-out then becomes like any other growing business, but the lessons learnt from buy-out and the often improved motivation of all concerned may give an added impetus to future development. The third element concerns exit by both the financing institutions and eventually by the management. An important area where problems may arise is in respect of the cohesion between members of the buy-out team. Whilst individual objectives may be suppressed at the time of the buy-out so as to ensure its success, these may arise again after the initial euphoria has subsided. Strains on the team may also arise where some members are not able to adapt fully to a new role which may involve a more strategic way of operating than had previously been the case. For most buy-outs these kinds of problem areas may be controllable but they do require attention in the fairly early stages of the buy-out. Exit routes, in particular, are a fundamental issue which must be addressed before the transfer of ownership takes place. As shown in this chapter, the buy-out market has now developed a variety of forms through which full or partial exit can be achieved. The appropriateness of these options to any particular buy-out requires careful assessment.

CHAPTER 9

Case studies

A consistent theme throughout this book has been an emphasis on the need to treat each prospective buy-out or buy-in on its merits. The precise details of each deal differ, but it is helpful to present illustrative cases. Not only do they demonstrate the feasibility of buying-out or buying-in – that is no longer in doubt – but they serve to highlight the nature of the problems that can provoke such a transaction in the first place, to illustrate the hurdles which may have to be surmounted to provide the basis for successful independent and sustained growth, and to demonstrate some of the eventual rewards that may accrue. Three case studies of buy-out on divestment and one buy-in are presented here. The first case shows how substantial reorganisation at the time of the buy-out to make the company independently viable can pay dividends in the longer term by providing the basis for a USM flotation. The second case relates to the divestment of local authority services to a buy-out team. The third involves divestment of activities in more than one country, which produces increased complexity in negotiations, financing and control. The fourth case illustrates the typical issues involved in a buy-in of a family owned firm.

Metsec plc: A buy-out on divestment achieving a USM quotation

Introduction
The buy-out of T.I. Metsec Ltd provides an interesting example of many of the issues that have been raised throughout this book. The company was bought out on divestment from the T.I. Group,

required a substantial amount of reorganisation and rationalisation and some four years later obtained a USM flotation. Since flotation the company has experienced further growth, both organically and via acquisition, and has subsequently reorganised itself into a divisionalised form. Each of these developments in the life cycle of Metsec plc is now discussed.

Origins
The original business was started in 1931 and was one of the first companies to engage in cold-roll forming in the UK. Independent existence the first time around did not last very long and in 1932 the company was acquired by Tube Investments. Over the next fifty years the business was developed to provide a wide product range for a variety of markets, building on their 'cold-rolling' expertise.

The period of recession in the early 1980s provided the environmental context for the buy-out. Poor performance caused the parent company T.I. to examine closely the future of its Metsec Company. With closure virtually the only other option, but with T.I. concerned to maintain its corporate image in its home region (both T.I. and Metsec are based in the West Midlands), a management buy-out was seen as an attractive alternative with the parent being very supportive of this option. Finance was obtained from 3i and ECI who were considered by the team to have been very helpful in alerting them to the possible problems to be faced in the future if much-needed rationalisation did not take place.

The buy-out took place in July 1981 for a price of under half a million pounds and with the buy-out team of five holding 60 per cent of the equity. The wider body of employees did not participate in funding the company at this time. It was in the consolidation stage shortly after the buy-out that a number of restructuring moves took place.

Consolidation: from buy-out to flotation
Given the poor trading circumstances that precipated the buy-out, a great deal of consolidation was required to stabilise the company as a viable independent entity. We may examine these changes under the general headings of product markets, employees and management and then assess their impact on performance in the period up to flotation in 1985.

Product markets Following the buy-out a marketing strategy was developed which drew on the commercial and technical strengths of the company which lay in the manufacture of products to customer requirements. As may be seen from Table 9.1 custom roll-formed products and construction-industry products contributed the bulk of sales turnover. Custom roll forming, using a variety of materials, is carried out to individual customer specifications. Customers for these products cover a wide range of sectors including up to 1985, building materials (18 per cent of sales), household products (13 per cent), electricals (12 per cent), transportation (10 per cent), leisure (19 per cent), construction (10 per cent) and retail stores (7 per cent). Within these markets the company was serving in 1985 about 150 regular customers, with no single customer representing more than 2 per cent of group turnover. Turnover in this product area grew substantially, on an annualised basis, from the buy-out to the time of the flotation. Competition in the industry was both from firms who compete across all sectors and from those smaller firms which focus on particular segments. Metsec plc achieved a 10 per cent share of the UK market and also performed strongly in the export market.

Construction-industry products, which form the largest single product group in the company at this time, are composed of purlins and side rails, lattice beams, and metframe. The first two are used as supports in industrial portal-frame-type buildings.

Metframe, developed after the buy-out from 1983 onwards, is a method of building based on pre-fabricated steel frame panels and is aimed at markets where speed of erection and cost effectiveness are important.

As with custom roll forming, construction-industry products are usually made to customer specifications, with the company's designers working closely with clients. A wide variety of customers are supplied for both purlins and lattice beams, with over 300

Table 9.1 Metsec product markets: turnover until the time of the flotation

	1982 (18 mths)		1983		1984		1985	
	(£000)	%	(£000)	%	(£000)	%	(£000)	%
Custom roll-formed products	3,353	31.4	2,989	36.0	3,763	30.3	–	–
Construction-industry products	7,329	68.6	4,998	60.3	8,268	66.7	14,387	96.7
Pneumatic-tube transfer systems	–	0	268	3.2	348	2.8	464	3.1
Business Systems	–	0	37	0.5	22	0.2	34	0.2
Total	10,682	100	8,292	100	12,401	100	14,885	100

customers being on the books in 1985 in respect of each product. Metsec is the market leader for both purlins and lattice beams. Competition in the former case comes from two major and six smaller competitors, with Metsec having increased its market share from 16 per cent to 27 per cent between 1981 and 1985. In the latter case competition comes from five smaller companies.

The remaining two product areas were introduced between the buy-out and flotation. In 1982 Metsec Business Systems was established to market computer systems which had been designed and installed within the company, and which were particularly concerned with stock control, production control and structural design.

Pneumatic tube conveyor systems were introduced following the acquisition of a major shareholding in a company specialising in this type of product. Although this activity is some way from traditional product areas, there is a logical link in terms of the existing business and administration skills within Metsec, especially in relation to contracting expertise. As with other product areas, a range of customer-specific products have been developed, focusing on cash-handling systems for the retail trade and the rapid transfer of documentation and components in other industries.

Employees Since the company was suffering from very poor performance in certain product areas at the time of the buy-out, a substantial redundancy programme was required as part of the process of re-positioning Metsec in the areas where it was most strongly placed. Out of a total workforce of 650 pre-buy-out, 470 were made redundant. A further ten redundancies were implemented in the first year after the buy-out so as to achieve the desired balance of employees across all product areas. From an initial post-buy-out workforce of 170 the company gradually took on labour, to reach 204 full-time employees at the end of 1985.

About half of these additional recruits came from those employed on temporary six-month contracts which are used to accommodate seasonal peaks in work-loads.

Management and employee relations As was seen in Chapters 3 and 8, having the right balance of capable management across all functions in the firm is crucial to securing backing for the buy-out in the first instance and for guiding its subsequent performance.

The Metsec buy-out team comprised five people, the managing

director, the technical director, the manufacturing director, the sales director and the commercial director. At the time of buy-out all were aged less than forty, providing a realistic expectation that the company should enjoy continuity of management. Their periods of service with Metsec ranged from three years to twenty-five years, although two members of the team had previously worked for the parent company for some years. The team therefore had a good balance of specific and general business experience and had worked together at Metsec within the parental group structure for three years before independence.

The next layer of management also had a good balance of age and experience. About half were aged less than thirty-five at the time of the buy-out with the rest generally btween forty-five to fifty-five. Most had been with the company for at least ten years though a handful of younger managers had been with Metsec for periods of less than five years.

Being employed either at parental group level or in a subsidiary of a group provided managers with an invaluable grounding in the discipline of financial and management control systems. However, the move from division to independent company required adjustments to the existing managerial structure so as to bring it into line with what was considered appropriate to the firm's new environment. A tier of management was removed and the organisation structure kept continuously under review in the light of new product developments which might require different managerial approaches.

With respect to employee relations, changes after the buy-out concerned a shift away from the specialised personnel department in the parent company to making line supervisors directly responsible for these issues. Additionally, communication with employees is now carried out formally through a works consultative council and a staff consultative council. Representatives on the council are generally drawn from the representatives of the most important trade union in each work area. An important feature of the constitution of these councils is that issues can only be taken outside the company for resolution where all parties agree, so placing emphasis on internally generated agreements. Throughout the negotiation phase and the period following the buy-out, employee relations were good. Because of the circumstances of the ownership transfer where closure was a very real possibility unless substantial rationalisation could be achieved, the buy-out was discussed in advance with the employees. Given this position, the poor alternative employment opportunities locally, and the higher-than-average wages, motivation of employees after the buy-out improved noticeably. The results of this increased motivation can be seen in the employee take-up rates following the USM flotation, which is discussed below, and in the financial performance of the company to which we now turn.

Performance between buy-out and flotation Post-buy-out performance can be examined in terms of profitability, liquidity and productivity; Table 9.2 provides some indicators on each of these aspects.

On an annualised basis both turnover and gross profits more than doubled in the period to flotation. Correspondingly, the gross profit to sales ratio also demonstrated an encouraging increase from 16.5 per cent at the start of the period to 20.8 per cent in 1985. Net profit levels in this period also showed remarkable growth.

Explanations for these developments lie both externally and internally. The external market-place was initially characterised by increasing competititon and pressure on profit margins. However, Metsec has benefited from the closure of at least two significant competitors, which removed excess capacity in the industry. Internally, the reorganisation following buy-out and the ending of a parental overhead burden contributed to a significant reduction in costs. Moreover, the rationalisation of production and the increased motivation in the workforce increased productivity levels. As may be seen from the table, the sales to employees ratio almost doubled up to 1985 whilst that for profits to employees increased thirty-fold.

Increases in debtors and creditors are to be expected as turnover increased so markedly, but the importance of strong internal control systems shows up clearly in the way that such increases were kept in line with sales growth. Nevertheless, by 1985 Metsec could see part of the advantages of a USM flotation as providing an increase in working capital availability in anticipation of continued rapid expansion.

The capital reorganisation and flotation
The capital reorganisation and the flotation on the USM by means of a Placing in October 1985 provided several benefits. First, the flotation gave the initial shareholders, both management and institutions, the opportunity to realise some of their investment. Second, the flotation enabled all employees to purchase shares and so participate in any future gains that Metsec might achieve. Third,

Table 9.2 Metsec post-buy-out performance

	1982 (18 mths)	1983	1984	1985	1986	1987	1988
Turnover (£000)	10,682	8,292	12,401	14,885	17,117	28,769	51,876
Gross profit (£000)	1,764	1,450	2,219	3,103	2,980	5,007	7,462
Gross profit/sales (%)	16.5	17.5	17.9	20.8	17.4	17.4	14.4
Net profit pre-interest (£000)	192	286	700	1,397	1,163	2,094	2,887
Pre-tax profit (£000)	162	253	658	1,380	1,131	2,023	2,776
Debtors/creditors	0.73	0.83	0.88	0.98	0.88	0.59	0.69
Sales/employee (£000)	40	47	65	75	75	80	86
Profits/employee (£000)	0.5	1.4	3.5	15.6	13.0	14.0	12.4

Source: Metsec plc Annual Report and Accounts (various).

the extra funds generated by the flotation reduced the gearing to a more reasonable level, provided additional working capital for expansion and gave the means to finance a large proportion of the purchase price of the freehold of the company's premises.

The effect of the USM Placing on Metsec's balance sheet is shown in Table 9.3. Essentially the capital reorganisation involved the redemption, cancellation and their redesignation as 10p Ordinary Shares of the Preference shares, the redesignation and subdivision as 10p Ordinary Shares of the Preferred Ordinary Shares, the subdivision of the Ordinary Shares into shares of 10p each and the creation of another 8.75 million Ordinary Shares of 10p each. The extra Ordinary Shares came into being by increasing the authorised share capital and crediting 8.75 million shares as fully paid by capitalising £875,000 of reserves; so as to give a new total of 12.5 million Ordinary Shares in issue. The Placing involved the sale of 3,812,500 Ordinary Shares at 67 pence per share, part of the

Table 9.3 Metsec balance sheets before and after USM placing as at 30 June 1985

	Before £		After £
Capital and reserves			
Called-up share capital		Called-up share capital	
50,000 12% cumulative		12.5m. ord. shares	
redeemable pref. shares of £1	50,000	of 10p.	1,250,000
100,000 12% cumulative			
convertible participating			
preferred ord. shares of £1	100,000		
150,000 Ord. shares of £1	150,000		
	300,000		
Revaluation reserve	173,000	*Share premium, reserve*	569,000
Profit and Loss a/c reserve	1,143,000	*Profit and loss a/c reserve*	441,000
	1,616,000		2,260,000
Fixed assets			
Tangible assets	915,000		1,665,000
Current assets			
Stock	803,000		803,000
Debtors	3,861,000		3,861,000
Cash	25,000		–
	4,689,000		4,664,000
Creditors (amounts falling due			
within one year)	(3,379,000)		(3,460,000)
Net current assets	1,310,000		1,204,000
Total assets less current liabilities	2,225,000		2,869,000
Creditors (amounts falling due			
after more than one year)	(361,000)		(361,000)
Provisions for liabilities and charges	(248,000)		(248,000)
	1,616,000		2,260,000

proceeds of which gives rise to the Share Premium Account of £569,000 in Table 9.3. With 30.5 per cent of the enlarged issued share capital of the company placed the management's equity stake reduced from 60 per cent to 48 per cent. The proceeds of the sale of the shares allowed them to repay the borrowings incurred at the time of the buy-out. The financing institutions (3i and ECI) reduced their shareholdings by 15 per cent but still retained a strong equity stake.

At the time of the buy-out only the five members of the core team had equity stakes in the business, with the managing director having a slightly larger stake than the other four members who each held identical stakes. On flotation all employees were encouraged to purchase shares at the placing price of 67 pence and some 60 per cent took advantage of the opportunity presented although the company did not extend loans to employees to enable them to buy shares. As at the time of the buy-out, the management team engaged in a major communications exercise, explaining the implications of the share issue to groups of employees on the shop floor. Additionally an Executive Share Option Scheme was introduced which covered full-time executive directors and other full-time employees selected by the Board of Directors. The maximum number of shares available under the scheme is 5 per cent of the issued Ordinary Share Capital. Apart from the shares acquired by the wider body of employees, 70 per cent of the shares floated on the USM were purchased by large institutions.

Post-flotation strategy and performance
Some of the elements of longer-term strategy have already been touched upon and relate to a twin approach involving organic growth based on expertise in traditional areas and acquisitions which complement the Group's business profile.

The purchase of the Air Tube Conveyors company has already been noted. Since flotation three other major acquisitions have been made. In July 1986, Energy Tubes Ltd, a specialist manufacturer of stainless-steel tubing was purchased with similar manufacturing techniques to the original cold-roll forming business of the Group. At the end of September 1987, the Thomas Vale Group was acquired. This company is involved in quality construction and related services such as plant hire and joinery, and is complementary to Metsec's Metframe business. In June 1988, Doc Con Systems was acquired so as to widen further the product base of Air Tube Conveyors into document handling.

Metsys Systems has also been developed from originally providing software and hardware to the Metsec Group to serving an
expanding external client base. Products include computerised
office control systems which can be integrated with production
equipment. These activities complement those of Air Tube Conveyors.

In order to accommodate these strategic developments, Metsec
plc was restructured at the end of 1987. The main trading activity
was transferred to Metal Sections Ltd, a wholly-owned subsidiary.
Metsec plc now provides Group services for strategic planning,
new-product development, training, management services and
treasury management. The Group consists of four divisions –
Building Products, Engineering Products (the original core business
of Metsec), Construction, and Electronic Products and Information
Control Systems. Correspondingly, the management teams in each
operational area have been reinforced, and have semi-autonomous
responsibility with main Board directors having a specific responsibility for a particular division.

Since flotation, and as a result of both internal growth and the
acquisitions described above, turnover and profits have increased
considerably (Table 9.2). The first year after flotation (1986) saw a
reversal in profit levels because of a decline in the industrial
building market; following the removal of capital allowances for
new buildings, which reduced demand for building products, as
well as strong competition in standard cold-roll forming products.
1987 and 1988 saw improved performance as a result of recovery in
these markets and a re-direction of emphasis on downstream
markets in the cold-roll forming areas in order to make best use of
Metsec's technical expertise. The introduction of further new
products and the continued growth of external client bases of
various activities which began as internal servicing functions also
contributed to growth. It is notable, however, that the process of
integration of the various activities is still continuing in order to
take best advantage of the complementarities between product
areas. Partly for these reasons the growth in sales has so far
outstripped that of profits producing a decline in gross profit to sales
and profits to employees ratios.

Available divisional information, which combines the Construction and Building Products divisions (Table 9.4) shows highest
profitability in Electronic Products though this sector is the smallest
within the company. Profits in Engineering Products declined in
1988, due to increased material costs, against increased turnover.

Table 9.4 Divisional performance of Metsec plc

	1988			1987		
	Turnover (£000)	Pre-tax profit (£000)	Profitability (%)	Turnover (£000)	Pre-tax profit (£000)	Profitability (%)
Construction and Building Products	35,179	1,746	5.0	15,889	1,030	6.5
Engineering Products	14,883	793	5.3	11,601	803	6.9
Electronic Products	1,814	237	13.1	1,279	190	14.9
Total	51,876	2,776	5.4	28,769	2,023	7.0

Source: Metsec plc Annual Report and Accounts (various).

The bulk of turnover and profits are contributed by the Construction and Building Products Divisions, which showed substantial growth in 1988 due to the influence of the Thomas Vale acquisition.

Employment which had increased to an average of 358 by 1987, rose sharply to 603 in 1988, reflecting, in part, acquisition activity. Further to encourage employee motivation and attachment to the company a Metsec Sharesave Scheme was introduced in 1989 to complement the existing Executive Share Option Scheme.

Conclusions

Metsec represents a classic case of an important aspect of management buy-outs. Here is a company required to break away from a parent group, needing substantial reorganisation to become viable but with this achieved, and the correct balance of the ingredients for success that this book has emphasised, able to achieve a USM flotation and to develop further as an independent group.

Here, too is another demonstration of what buy-outs involve – the desire on the part of management to pursue an independent existence. In order for this independence to be maintained the persistence of an entrepreneurial spirit is required.

City Centre Leisure: A local authority buy-out

Introduction

The growing number of buy-outs on the privatisation of local authority services was seen in Chapters 1 and 2. The case of City Centre Leisure, which involved a management team winning a tender to run two out of the five indoor leisure centres owned by The City of Westminster, illustrates the issues involved in this form of buy-out.

Background

Almost all local authority services are run by local authority departments employing their own staff. Leisure services, sport and recreation and the management of leisure centres are no exception to that rule.

In summer 1987, The City of Westminster decided to add the management of its five indoor leisure centres to its existing list of services to be subject to competitive tendering in advance of formal

Government legislation. The aim was to seek tenders early in 1988 with contracts to commence in September 1988.

The tender was for the management of one or all of the five leisure centres and was based on deficit funding. The specification included requests for suggestions on reducing the deficit whilst improving the services and demanded an estimated cost (the difference between estimated income and actual costs) for five years, for each centre, together with reductions which might result from consolidated adjustments. Responsibilities for assets such as the building or equipment were not included.

In early 1988, City Centre Leisure was established as a company by the then Assistant Director of Leisure of City of Westminster Council and three colleagues. Funding requirements were identified for professional fees and set-up costs, as well as for the funding of debtors. (The City of Westminster provides deficit funding monthly in arrears.) Since the tender was not to include purchase of property, facilities or equipment, the funding requirement was quite modest and comprised £50,000 equity from the Directors, secured on personal guarantees and assets, together with an initial £100,000 clearing-bank overdraft facility.

The management of City Centre Leisure carefully selected the most appropriate staff from the City of Westminster's Leisure Department as the complement of people required to own the new operation. These staff were not offered equity in the new company, but were offered better terms of employment than those offered by the City of Westminster. Changes included a reduction in the basic hours of work, a pension scheme, the introduction of a bonus scheme based on centre performance, and marginally better holidays. The previous sickness benefit scheme was, however, reduced.

In the event, City Centre Leisure was successful, against severe competition, in being awarded the contract for the management of two of the five centres, the Queen Mother Sports Centre in Victoria and the Seymour Leisure Centre in Marylebone. The £2,590,300 contract was awarded for a period of five years.

Post buy-out

In the first six months after buy-out some 27,000 more people used the facilities of the two leisure centres compared to the same period in the previous year. The increases included a 26 per cent volume growth in swimming, 65 per cent in aerobics, and 35 per cent in the fitness room.

This level of growth is attributed to certain factors relating to the buy-out itself. First, charges were not increased in this period. Second, opportunities to use the facilities have been increased through longer opening hours and a more flexible programme, particularly in the mornings, evenings and at weekends. Third, action has been taken to improve certain aspects of the service following a user survey. Fourth, customer-care training and encouragement have been introduced with further efforts planned in this direction. In addition to these factors, management report themselves to be clearer and sharper about what they are trying to do than before the buy-out. Moreover, the attitudes and interest levels of the staff are also reported to have improved, with consequences for the quality of service provided. Plans for the development of City Centre Leisure are initially to better the cost targets set in the tender and to share any over-achievement of those targets with the Council.

The Business Plan for the two centres, included a major capital improvement programme of facilities. Thirteen projects were identified and the work was due for completion by the end of 1989. Funding for this development programme was arranged via a £750,000 medium-term bank loan, guaranteed by the City of Westminster.

Future development of the business is seen in diversification outside the City of Westminster, winning other leisure centre management contracts; and probably working in other closely related areas. A four-year Business Plan came into operation on 1 September 1989.

The operation of the contract
The nature and conditions of the contract are key to the local authority ensuring that an adequate level of service is provided and in enabling the buy-out team to develop the business.

In late 1989 the local authority were reported to be satisfied so far with the new arrangements: in terms of the quality of service being offered, the cost savings which accrue to the council and its ratepayers, and the reduction in control problems in managing the leisure centres. Ultimate responsibility for the leisure centres does, however, rest with the local authority and the new arrangements mean a change in the way its monitoring role is carried out.

Issues relating to the specification of the contract concern five main factors – restrictions, flexibility, charges, publicity, and penalty points. For a dynamic industry such as leisure, management consider that the contract is too restrictive and does not provide enough flexibility. Negotiations over charges remain rigid, with it being necessary to await a committee cycle or even a council year to effect changes. City Centre Leisure is also still required to clarify and check with the Council all the simple factors about producing publicity material before it can be sent out. From the Council's point of view, the penalty-points aspect of the contract may not be as effective as it could be. The existence of two contractors may also increase the Council's monitoring costs but it does provide the Council with a basis for comparisons. There is the possibility that a desire to maintain equitability may restrict initiative but having two contractors can provide the Council with some security should one fail to perform.

Conclusions

At the time of writing it is still too early to make final conclusions about the benefits of this type of buy-out, although initial indications are highly positive. This particular case was the first of its kind and some of the contractual issues identified may be refined and resolved in subsequent buy-outs. These issues are particularly noteworthy given the concern expressed in the Audit Commissioner's paper, published in early 1990, about this kind of buy-out. An important element in the success of the buy-out is likely to be the successful transition by management and staff from the culture of being local authority employees to running an independent business, whilst maintaining an enhanced awareness to provide value-for-money service quality. Professionalism, personal commitment and business understanding are essential ingredients of this process of change.

The management of City Centre Leisure have also identified the need to diversify their activities as a means of reducing dependence upon one limited life contract.

Vickers Furniture (VF) International: a cross-border management buy-out

Introduction

An aspect of corporate restructuring may commonly be the decision to divest completely a particular set of a group's activities. Whilst this repositioning may once have involved the sale of small peripheral activities, more recent action may involve much larger divisions or business units which had previously been an important strategic element of the parent. These business units often involve operations based in several countries. The strategic decision to sell means not simply divesting those activities furthest away geographically from the parent's home country, but disposal of the whole set. In pursuing such a policy a parent may face the choice of disposal in one transaction or break-up of the business unit and sale to several purchasers. Whichever route is chosen will be influenced by the homogeneity of the activities, their coherence as an independent activity, or their fit with a potential trade purchaser, which in turn will determine the optimum price to be realised. Sales of activities which span several countries may raise complex problems, particularly for completion of a buy-out. The case of Vickers Furniture International illustrates these various aspects of cross-border buy-outs.

Background
The UK business of Vickers Furniture began over fifty years ago as a filing cabinet maker, based in Dartford. The Vickers Furniture division was created in the early 1980s, following an internal reorganisation of Vickers. By the late 1980s it was one of the four largest suppliers of office-system furniture in the UK with an overall market share of 9 per cent, but with 27 per cent of the 'prime' office furniture market and with certain specialist products being market leaders.

Vickers had acquired the old-established Roneo business in France in 1969. Since 1945 this company had become a significant steel-furniture manufacturer. In 1975 Behin-Robustacier Meubles (BRM) a manufacturer of wood office furniture was also acquired. The French operation became a manufacturer of desking and seating, storage and filing products and systems-based furniture, with about 10 per cent of the market. The UK and French operations operate in separate market segments.

In 1985, C. A. Parsons of Ireland, a storage-products manufacturer and importer was acquired. The furniture division also included an operation based in Germany, but this relied heavily on exports to the US and was sold separately to a US buyer.

The performance of Vickers Furniture prior to the buy-out is shown in Table 9.5. Turnover increased comfortably throughout the period, with gross profits increasing at a slower rate, producing a downturn in the gross profit to turnover ratio in 1987 and 1988. Net profits before and after interest were uneven throughout the period, although the 1988 levels show marked signs of recovery.

In terms of contribution by the three main elements of the group, the majority of turnover (57 per cent) is provided by Vickers Roneo in France, with the UK operations accounting for 41 per cent and the

Table 9.5 VF International Ltd: profit and loss
accounts 1984–1988

	1984	1985	1986	1987	1988
Turnover (£m.)	60.8	65.3	76.1	78.3	85.0
Increase (%)	–	7.4	16.5	2.9	8.6
Cost of sales (£m.)	36.9	39.3	45.2	47.6	52.9
Increase (%)	–	6.5	15.0	5.3	11.1
Gross profit (£m.)	23.9	26.0	30.9	30.7	32.1
Gross profit/turnover (%)	39.4	39.8	40.3	39.6	37.8
Profit, pre-interest (£m.)	3.4	2.8	3.8	3.7	4.4
Profit, post-interest (£m.)	2.1	1.4	1.9	1.9	2.4

Source: Annual Report and Accounts.

small Irish site the balance of 2 per cent. Profit contributions, have until recently been in the opposite direction, with Vickers Furniture in the UK returning greater profits than Vickers Roneo in the ratio approximately two to one. The UK operation has approximately 1,000 employees, with the slightly larger French business 1,300.

These patterns of performance of the group are related to the need for reorganisation of the UK operations which began in 1987 and which involved substantial capital expenditure. Capital-expenditure needs also had a marked adverse impact upon cash flow at this time. Much of this work had been completed before the buy-out, with the benefits beginning to be shown in the accounts in 1988. However, further investment was required and the financial structure put in place at the time of the buy-out had to make allowance for this need. Nevertheless, unless macro-economic conditions were to suffer a significant downturn with a consequent effect on office furniture purchasers, it was considered that the UK operation was well placed for growth. Key features of the strategy for growth were an emphasis on customer service and the development of European sales through the links between the UK and French operations which would permit cross-selling of products. Following major reorganisation of Vickers Roneo, including the installation of a new management team after several years of instability, it was considered that the French side of the group was now in a good position for future development.

The buy-out
Vickers plc took the strategic decision in 1987 to exit from office-furniture markets. Senior management of Vickers Furniture subsequently spent a considerable period trying to find buyers for the business, either as a whole or for the three almost stand-alone parts

in France, Germany and the UK. During this period another management team within the company began to prepare a buy-out attempt. As noted earlier, the German part of the business was sold to a US Group. Whilst there were serious bidders for the other activities, only the buy-out attempt which was eventually successful was trying to buy both Vickers Furniture and Vickers Roneo. As such, it offered the vendor a less complex sale, although completing a cross-border buy-out introduced its own complexities. These difficulties were compounded by the late stage in the process at which the successful buy-out attempt began. The leader of the buy-out team had agreed not to undertake any buy-out attempt without the approval of the vendors whilst the process of sale was in progress. Once the process began in earnest it was necessary to divide responsibilities between those managers who would be involved in negotiating the transaction and those who would concentrate on continuing to run the business.

Given the time constraints, it was seen as an advantage to link with a financing institution which could lead the deal and provide both equity and debt finance, a role that was fulfilled by Security Pacific Hoare Govett Equity Ventures. However, syndication of the finance was also required. An important aspect of the financing arrangements was the need to pre-syndicate the equity to establish the buy-out vehicle as a majority European Community-owned holding company, thus enabling consent to be gained from the French Ministry of Finance for the transfer of ownership of Vickers Roneo.

The need to deal with different taxation and legal regimes between the UK and France, and the issues involved in conducting due diligence in two countries added to the complexity of the deal. Further difficulties required resolution in respect of management and financiers in the two countries.

Given the much less developed buy-out market in France, as noted in Chapter 1, the management of Vickers Roneo were much less familiar than their UK colleagues with what it entailed. Not the least of their concerns related to management warranties. French management were also concerned about the introduction of another foreign owner. The recent managerial changes in France and the involvement of French management in the buy-out team meant that these problems were overcome. At a late stage in the process one of the participating banks in Vickers Roneo's working-capital facilities withdrew. However, this institution was replaced by the Unicredit subsidiary of Crédit Agricole, which also took on the lead bank role in France. This change also helped deal with problems arising from differences in familiarity with buy-outs between French institutions. Despite agreeing the purchase in March 1988 it took until November of that year for physical completion to occur. The final financial structure for the transaction which was completed at a discount to net assets is shown in Table 9.6. As noted earlier, the capital expenditure programme was not complete at the time of the buy-out and the financing structure needed to take account of future requirements. The use of deferred consideration in the form of a vendor loan for £7.5m. helped resolve this problem but was a factor in the delayed completion.

A key aspect of the financial structure was that the equity stake of management and employees, as is quite common in larger deals, was related to a ratchet mechanism. In this case, the ratchet is related to the market capitalisation of Vickers Furniture on a trade sale or flotation any time within five years of the completion of the buy-out. Management and employees' equity holding is permitted to increase once the institutional rate of return has achieved a given level in percentage terms. If sale or flotation does not occur within this period, the ratchet will operate on an agreed capital value at

Table 9.6 Vickers Furniture financial structure

	£m.
Equity*	5.3
Vendor loan	7.5
Overdrafts	
UK	2.5
France	9.5
Medium-term loan	15.5
Total	40.3
Funding requirements	
Purchase price	27.0
Existing French debt	9.5
Overdraft UK	2.5
Costs & expenses	1.3
	40.3

* Equity was divided as follows:- SPHG Equity Ventures and Mercury Asset Management (18.86 per cent each); Charterhouse D.C., CIN Industrial Investments, Citicorp Capital Investors Europe, County Natwest Ventures and Phildrew Ventures (10.18 per cent each) and employees and management (11.38 per cent). Management and employee's equity was issued in two stages, one at the time of the buy-out and one several months afterwards.

the end of five years. The maximum that management and employees can achieve under the provisions of the ratchet is approximately 40 per cent of the equity.

At the time of writing it is a little early to comment on post-buy-out performance, although the company has been able to repay some loans ahead of schedule. A flotation is planned for 1992.

Conclusions

This case has illustrated the nature of the issues which might arise where a buy-out involves subsidiaries of relatively equal import-ance in different countries. Besides the normal problems of dealing with a vendor, new difficulties relating to the different perspectives of management and financing institutions, and varying legal and taxation environments need to be resolved. The willingness to purchase cross-border activities can be an advantage in relation to the vendor who is offered a less complex sale. The extent of other problems may be diminished in respect of future deals as buy-outs become more widely known in continental Europe and legal and taxation frameworks become more harmonised. Nevertheless, such developments are likely to take time and seem unlikely to remove completely all problems. An important issue appears to be the need to reassure management in the countries concerned that they are an important element in the success of such buy-outs and to recognise, where appropriate, that decentralisation of management between countries but within a common strategy may be ben-eficial.

Innoxa: A management buy-in of a family-owned firm

Introduction

As the trends reviewed in Chapter 1 showed, management buy-ins have become a significant part of the overall buy-out market. There are many similarities between buy-outs and buy-ins, particularly in respect of financing structures. However, there are also significant differences as this case demonstrates. Most importantly, manage-ment wishing to buy-in have to find the target and assess it from the outside using publicly available information. In a buy-out, the target is already known and management at least ought to have detailed knowledge of the business. The need to thoroughly appraise the business is important since a key characteristic of buy-ins is a requirement to turnround a company which is underperforming. These issues are illustrated in the buy-in of Innoxa, where considerable effort was required to identify problem areas prior to the transaction being finalised.

The buy-in entrepreneur

Typically a buy-in may be expected to involve the introduction of a new senior management team covering the main functional areas. In this case, the buy-in team consisted of one individual entrepreneur who had founded and ran Suriplan, a small cosmetics business in Streatham. Suriplan had developed and subsequently produced and marketed the 'Packa' range of personal hygiene products. The range was designed for travellers and comprised miniaturised toiletry products, shaving equipment, shampoo and deodorants. Agreement had been reached by which Boots the Chemist would become sole distributors of the Packa range in the United Kingdom.

The target

Innoxa was formed in 1920 and had become a well-known supplier of products to the mature woman sector of the cosmetics market. By the late 1980s the company had developed into an international group but remained under family ownership. The group has an established brand name and operations in the United Kingdom, Australia, New Zealand, South Africa, Germany and Sweden. Innoxa also has distribution facilities in Japan. The company's three principal brands are Innoxa itself, Leichner and Dorothy Gray. The main distribution outlet in the United Kingdom is Boots and the company's name is synonymous with allergy-free products. Pre-tax profits to the end of June 1988, the year immediately prior to the buy-in, were £0.4million as against £0.3million the previous year (Table 9.7). Turnover was £15.1million compared with £14.2 million in 1987. Borrowings had increased by 10 per cent between 1987 and 1988 to £3.3million.

The buy-in

The entrepreneur's motive for undertaking a buy-in was to achieve growth ambitions more easily than was possible through expanding existing business activities. Innoxa became available for acquisition in June 1988 as the family shareholders sought a buyer to reinvigorate the company's brand image.

Whilst Innoxa had attractions as a suitable buy-in target, there were several problem areas. These difficulties are not untypical of a

Table 9.7 Innoxa Ltd: summarised financial
information (£m.)

	1987	1988
Profit and loss account		
Turnover	14.2	15.1
Operating profit	1.0	1.1
Interest	0.7	0.7
Profit before taxation	0.3	0.4
Tax	0.1	–
Profit after taxation	0.2	0.4
Balance sheet		
Net assets	2.6	3.0
Borrowing	3.0	3.3
Cash flow		
Cash generated from operations	0.6	0.6
Net capital expenditure	(1.1)	(0.5)
Tax and dividend payments	(0.1)	(0.1)
Absorbed by working capital	–	(0.3)
Net increase in borrowing	(0.6)	(0.3)

buy-in of a private company. In all deals of this type there is a need
to arrive at a sale price which will be both acceptable to the vendor
and fundable by venture and other forms of borrowings. For
external providers of finance to be willing to invest in such a deal
they have to be convinced that the calibre of management and the
earnings stream of the company are high enough to produce returns
which will meet their targets. The problem in a buy-in, unlike a
buy-out, is that the management who wish to effect the deal do not
have access to detailed information about the company. Reliance
has to be placed on thorough analysis of publicly available information. It is here that experienced advisers can have a key role to play.

The buy-in entrepreneur together with his advisers undertook a
detailed analysis of Innoxa in order to identify its strengths and
weaknesses and arrive at a sensible offer price. Given the
geographical spread of business activities, this examination required access to industry and business statistics in several countries.
From an analysis of general market statistics and a comparison of
Innoxa with other similar cosmetics companies, the following
major areas of concern were identified. The company's gross
margins were too low and its overheads were too high. Hence,
despite the advantages of the brand name, net profitability was
considerably below what it might have been. Cash flow was also
adversely affected by excessively high stock and debtor levels. It
was also evident that Innoxa had serious marketing problems.

Packaging was poor and old-fashioned. Marketing efforts were not properly focused and were being held back by the company's technical orientation. The marketing skills of the buy-in entrepreneur could thus make a strong contribution to the turnround of the company.

On the basis of the information gathered an outline business plan was produced. It was felt that this plan could be defended as realistic. Institutional support was obtained for the proposal with the development capital firm suggesting an appropriate financing structure.

Negotiations with the vendor involved both financial and emotional considerations. As is frequently the case in this kind of deal, there was a need to reassure the vendor that the family business was being handed on to someone who was going to preserve and expand it as an independent entity. Agreement was reached on a price of £4million on condition that the company's net assets did not fall below £3million. The price represented a goodwill element on net assets of one third and was perceived by both sides to be fair. A further four months of detailed investigation and research were required to complete the acquisition. This process involved the development of detailed business plans to justify the acquisition and identify future strategy. The group structure was examined carefully to identify tax planning opportunities, to plan funding of the group and to minimise the impact of exchange rate fluctuations. Marketing plans needed to be rewritten and new internal structures and control systems established. Stock control was improved and group purchasing initiatives were established.

Product ranges were reviewed and new pricing strategies were developed. As a result of this process, revised financial forecasts were presented to the supporting investors.

The financing structure of the combined activities of Innoxa and Suriplan is shown in Table 9.8 and involved £4million of debt at a

Table 9.8 Innoxa Ltd: financing structure

	£m.
Convertible ordinary shares – management	0.27
Cumulative redeemable participating preferred ordinary shares – institution	0.40
Total equity	0.67
Convertible unsecured loan stock 1993	4.00
Total	4.67

fixed interest rate of 11 per cent. The buy-in entrepreneur exchanged his shares in Suriplan for 40 per cent of the shares in the new company, with the balance being held by the development capital institution.

The buy-in entrepreneur's equity stake was subject to a ratchet agreement of the kind described in earlier chapters. Providing that the debt was repaid according to a pre-agreed schedule and that a target capitalisation of the group could be achieved either by flotation or trade sale within five years, the buy-in entrepreneur's shareholding would increase to 64 per cent. Failure to achieve these targets could reduce the equity stake to 25 per cent. Between these two points, the ratchet operated on a sliding scale according to the extent to which these targets were met.

Post buy-in

Since the buy-in was completed several operational and managerial changes have been made. The Innoxa manufacturing plant at Eastbourne has been rationalised and efficiency has been improved. The whole range of products has been repackaged and a major new range is being introduced. Stock and debtor levels were reduced and operating overheads cut. Management changes have included improved motivation as a result of the change in ownership. Outside the United Kingdom, internal and external promotions have been made in South Africa and Australia, respectively, to enhance the calibre of senior management.

Turnover in the first year after the buy-in increased to £16million. Despite the costs and transition problems caused by the changes implemented throughout the group, profits before the costs of funding the acquisition rose to £1million.

Conclusions

The amount of effort required to put together a credible management buy-in proposal is considerable. It is exacerbated by the restricted availability of information about the target company and the incumbent management team. As buy-ins often arise in turnround situations it is crucial to identify problem areas as fully as possible prior to completion of the deal.

CHAPTER 10

Prospects for buy-outs and buy-ins

From being virtually unknown in 1980, management buy-outs became a phenomenon of the decade, answering in the affirmative the question posed at the very first National Buy-out Conference held at Nottingham in 1981: 'Management Buy-outs, Corporate Trend for the 80s?'. Together with the more recent but related management buy-in, the value of the slightly over five hundred deals completed in 1989 was £7.5 billion. The value of the buy-in market is now almost equal to that for buy-outs. This level of activity accounts for 25 per cent of the total value of the whole take-over market and 33.3 per cent of the volume of transactions. That buy-outs and buy-ins would become so significant was difficult to imagine in 1980.

From their initial growth in the recessionary period of 1981 and 1982, buy-outs were widely welcomed as a key factor in saving jobs and re-invigorating both the parent companies who divested subsidiaries to management teams and the bought-out firms themselves. This view prevailed throughout much of the 1980s until the gloss of buy-outs became tarnished in the eyes of some commentators by a small number of protracted take-over battles involving stock-market deals, their association with high levels of debt, and the operating problems of several high-profile buy-outs in a period of exceptionally high real interest rates which has seriously affected certain sectors after several years of rapid growth. Attention has also been focused on doubts about the performance of buy-outs and on the notion that buy-outs have become just a financial engineering exercise offering management and institutions substantial returns in a very short period presumably at the cost of the former shareholders.

In view of these question marks surrounding buy-outs it is appropriate in this concluding chapter to assess their prospects in the 1990s.

Performance

Perhaps the best-known survey to report performance improvements in buy-outs was the study carried out for KKR of a sample of its investments. The report was treated with a degree of scepticism, particularly given some more recent well-publicised difficulties with parts of the KKR portfolio. Were this the only study of buy-out performance to show marked performance improvements then there would quite rightly have been grounds for doubt if not disbelief. However, there have now been some 25 studies of buy-outs on both sides of the Atlantic published in serious academic books and journals. These studies have covered virtually all aspects of buy-out performance, including rises in share price following the announcement of a buy-out in the case of quoted company deals, increases in profitability, cost-cutting, reorganisation, employment, capital expenditure, research and development, cash flow, advertising expenditure, taxation benefits and short-term versus long-term improvements.

In the US, positive developments have been recorded in respect of most aspects of firm performance by all studies. The exceptions relate to mixed results in respect of capital expenditure and R&D. Employment levels have tended to fall initially then rise after buy-out. Studies by CMBOR, reported in earlier chapters and elsewhere, together with a limited amount of other UK research would broadly support the US evidence, especially in the early years after buy-out. There are few studies which show disappointing post-buy-out performance and some of those which do are not robust enough to add significant weight to the debate. Hence, for example a US study of declines in R&D etc., was based on a few case studies and a recent UK study of long-term performance in buy-outs which showed performance returning to industry norms in the long term after having achieved short-term improvements has to be treated with care, again because of the small sample involved. Many buy-outs have traditionally been in mature industries and frequently enjoyed special market-niche positions and so cannot necessarily be expected to enjoy high long-term rates of growth. Until more long-term studies of buy-outs are available, it is thus premature to form a final judgement.

Short- versus long-term ownership firms

The significant number of deals which have either been sold or floated within a few years after buy-out, as seen in Chapter 8, has raised questions about whether buy-outs are a long-term owner-ship form or merely a means of financial engineering to give the new shareholders significant short-term capital gains. It is true that about 15 per cent of all buy-outs have now exited by means of either a trade sale or flotation. Some 40 per cent of buy-outs transacted for prices in excess of £25m. have exited in an average time of around three years. However, the corollary is that the vast majority of buy-outs still retain their original ownership structure. These buy-outs are generally the smaller principally development-capital- or clearing-bank-backed firms where management have a majority of the equity. It was this kind of deal, very different from the large buy-outs with more significant elements of debt finance, which was originally seen as the vehicle for a new longer-term form of ownership structure. However, there are also a significant number of large heavily debt-financed buy-outs where a long-term perspective is envisaged in the financial structure.

Even where a long-term involvement was initially expected, changing market circumstances and opportunities for the firm may require a reassessment of this position. As was pointed out in Chapter 8, there is an encouraging growth in the methods by which realisations can be effected. For many buy-outs, it is perfectly possible that restructuring needs to be organised within a relatively short time to provide funds for further growth whilst maintaining the essence of a buy-out structure. This point also needs to be seen within the context of the high levels of corporate restructuring which have occurred through takeover activity since the mid-1980s and the emphasis for strategic success on ranking within a market. There may, thus be sound reasons for seeking a friendly acquisition. There is a serious danger in taking a static view of buy-out structures. A buy-out which does not adjust to the opportunities available may begin to underperform. Those which change may be the high performers in industries with a need to obtain considerably more outside funding or a much greater critical mass in order to pass on to the next stage in the corporate life cycle.

These possibilities for longer-term re-leveraging or additional finance for acquisitions highlight the changing attitudes to the use of debt in an initial buy-out structure. The gearing levels in UK buy-outs increased significantly in the last three years of the 1980s with the growing availability of mezzanine debt, more aggressive attempts by senior debt players to establish a strong market presence and the need, given high transaction prices, for equity investors to achieve their traditional returns. UK deals remain much less highly geared than their US counterparts with lower reliance on mezzanine finance.

High levels of debt and institutional behaviour

It is misleading to see the problems reported in late 1989 in some very large buy-outs as spelling doom for the market as a whole. Most companies involved are in sectors which have traditionally been susceptible to cyclical demand patterns, and have seen earlier buy-out failures, even though they are cash-flow businesses. Many less leveraged companies in these sectors which are not buy-outs have also encountered severe problems after several successful years. It must be stressed that high levels of debt are most appropriate in stable industries which are resistant to cyclical downturns and where cash flows can be virtually guaranteed. It may be that the possibility for downturns was unrealistically played down against a background of historically fast economic growth at a time when attention was focused on the issue of paying outgoing owners a fair price. It is also necessary to consider what might have happened in the absence of an MBO. Arguably, under the previous ' ownership regime (such as being a quoted company) the position could have deteriorated further before action was taken. In buy-outs, the high levels of debt with strict covenants and highly focused institutional monitoring should identify problems earlier and allow viable alternative plans to be adopted even if in difficult circumstances and with much higher personal pressures on management than might otherwise be the case.

It has not just been the increasing absolute level of gearing and problem cases which have given rise to concern. For example, an important feature of recent developments has been aggressive fee-driven deal completion by some lead institutions who then syndicate down most of the debt to leave themselves with a relatively small exposure and the ability to pursue further deals. This raises questions about the commitment of the deal leader in such circumstances to the performance of the buy-out, particularly if the deal is perceived to go wrong. Deal leaders may in future retain higher proportions of debt in large deals in order to be able to convince other institutions to participate in syndication. There does not seem to be a great deal of evidence that this is happening; a view that is not encouraged by warnings by US regulators to US banks against investing in European buy-outs because of the increased risk due to a lesser ability than in the US to sell down debt.

How well-diversified syndicate members are in terms of their portfolio of buy-out investments is by no means clear. Some banks are likely to have inadequately diversified portfolios and may have taken relatively large tranches of a very small number of deals. One reason for such an approach may relate to the transactions costs involved in assessing whether an investment should be made or not. If costs of appraisal are high and indivisible, it may be considered appropriate to take the view that an investment is either made or it is not, rather than reducing the amount advanced. Institutions ought accordingly to trade-off the level of risk with the pricing of finance. There are current indications that the margins above London Inter-bank Offer Rate (LIBOR) sought on senior debt have risen. The returns looked for on mezzanine debt have also increased, closing the gap between this type of instrument and equity. These rates are also inversely related to the scale of financing involved. In the current environment of caution with few deals being completed one cannot be very sure that the higher rates being sought are actually being achieved. Hence, one may still envisage a position whereby large amounts are being lent at relatively low prices.

The overall buy-out market must be seen in the context of its very wide spread of deal values, from transactions involving a few hundred thousand pounds to the high-value controversial cases such as Magnet and Isosceles. Within this range there is a wide variety of investors and deals. Many small and medium-sized transactions have debt/equity ratios of no more than 3:1 and may need only one investor for each type of financing instrument, thus avoiding the public problems of syndication. Additionally in this area of the market, and especially for buy-outs from privately owned companies, prices may be influenced by factors other than those which are acceptable to stock-market analysts. Thus a safer overall financial structure may emerge, but one which must take account of the basic principles of buy-out finance – cash-flow stability, strong competitive position, market niche, strong management, etc. The ability to effect such transactions in a hostile environment will depend heavily on management taking independent professional advice at a very early stage in the buy-out process.

Prospects

As we look to the prospects for buy-outs in the 1990s, the market in the short term reflects different pressures – large leveraged deals, especially going privates, are difficult to achieve and for institutions to syndicate. This is not to say that such buy-outs are unworkable, but that in the short term they are more likely to reflect special circumstances such as a major shareholder who had taken the company public in the 1980s wishing to take it private again. Such deals may not be more generally favoured until interest rates decline and the threat of a recession recedes.

Small and medium-sized buy-outs are dependent on different factors for success and as such can survive against a less favourable economic background. Indeed, the buy-outs of the early 1980s which paved the way for the expansion of the market in the mid-1980s, were completed during a deep recession. Buy-outs are now an accepted part of corporate restructuring.

Renewed recessionary pressures and high interest rates are likely to bring pressure on groups to divest at prices which are attractive to management teams. A slowing down of economic activity, even if a recession does not materialise, will reinforce the need for firms to examine the spread of their interests. If the acquisitive behaviour of firms begins to ease, the attractiveness of buy-outs will be strengthened. In addition, privatisation of areas such as local-government services and ancillary health services is set to provide a significant number of buy-outs. Buy-ins are also becoming more important although major problems remain in matching management teams to suitable targets. The divestment of subsidiaries to buy-in teams has begun to emerge as a significant alternative to the buy-out.

The quality of institutions and advisers is likely to play a more important role than in the 1980s. The less certain circumstances forecast for the early 1990s may involve institutions in a more active monitoring role than was generally appropriate in the late 1980s. There will be an increasing divide between those institutions looking for relatively short-term returns and those prepared to stay with the buy-out for up to ten years. Within this timescale, however, institutions may obtain returns from redemptions of certain classes of shares, share buy-backs and recapitalisations rather than the traditional routes of flotation or trade sale. At the same time the ratchets introduced in the middle to late 1980s continue to prove controversial.

The 1990s are also likely to see an internationalisation of the European buy-out market as institutions in various countries engage in reciprocal deal investments with an accompanying simplification of the procedures for effecting pan-European buy-outs. This development may lead to a more European orientated post-buy-out acquisition and growth strategy. Buy-outs, then, will continue to play an important role in corporate restructuring.

Index